Overcast

Bill Wheatley

"Overcast," by Bill Wheatley. ISBN 978-1-62137-865-5 (softcover). Published 2016 by Virtualbookworm.com Publishing Inc., P.O. Box 9949, College Station, TX 77842, US. ©2016, Bill Wheatley.

All rights reserved. No part of this publication may be reproduced, stored in a retrieval system, or transmitted in any form or by any means, electronic, mechanical, recording or otherwise, without the prior written permission of Bill Wheatley.

Overcast
a collection of verse

Bill Wheatley

In memory of
Beth Kodama

Contents

1. **CHILDREN OF SYRACUSE** 1
    - Overcast 3
    - Children of Syracuse 4
    - Baby Teeth 10
    - Becoming a Parent 13
    - Danny Boy 15
    - The Fat Lady of the Midway 16
    - Query 19
    - Harry Victor White 20
    - Hammer Throw 21
    - G-Man 23
    - Tuxedo Junction 26
    - Driving, Speed 29
    - Unborn 31
    - North Wind 32
    - A Wish 33
    - At Sixty-Eight 35
    - Shameless Thing 38
2. **BETH** 41
    - Bald 43
    - First Look 44
    - A Second Look 45
    - Clairvoyant 46
    - Possession 47
    - The Meninges 48
    - The Mole 50
    - Native Archetype 53
    - Seized 54
    - Betrayal 56
    - Rhymes With 59
    - Chadao 61
    - Hurricane Brain 62
    - Twenty-third Psalm 65
    - An Unwarranted Sense of Well-Being 66
    - Unwritten Story 68
    - Twins 70
    - Last Day 73
    - The Puakenikeni Tree 74
    - Elephantine 75

    Purgatory Fantasy 77
    Wondering 79
3.   OUTSIDE WORLD 81
    The Perfect Tomato 83
    Nostalgia 84
    Twig 85
    Grammatical Incident 87
    Dashing Andy 88
    Wildlife Porn 89
    Glock 92
    Micicide 94
    The Strad 96
    Trinity 97
    Vietnam Memorial 101
    lower case man 105
    Already Dead 107
    One Three Hundred-Millionth 109
    Super Bowl XLV 112
4.   FRIENDS, OTHERS 115
    The Unadvertised End 117
    Lily 118
    Bullshit 120
    Happy Birthday, Josef 122
    Friends' Sweaters 123
    Permission 127
    Ex 133
    The Graph of Love 137
    Yet Again 139
    Battle Fatigue 142
    Unmoored 144
    Therapy Dog 146
    Magic 147
    Russian Poetry 149
    Compost Heap 151
    Grunts, Clicks 153
    Respect 156

1. Children of Syracuse

Overcast

The sky hangs very low
I don't know why

some meteorological effect
I don't know why

If you stand on the high hill
beside Loretto Rest

where Louise died
the city there below

it feels as if the sky
is looming overhead

and I always think
it might be Russia.

Syracuse has the most
sunless days and highest

average annual snowfall
of any city in the world

with a population over
one hundred thousand.

Children of Syracuse

A pebble dropped in Onondaga Lake sends ripples out
    to lap on Syracuse, New York,
on Siracusa, Sicily, where rippling back in time Dionysius
    the Elder ruled
what Cicero called the most beautiful city in the world,
    the one where
Archimedes bathed and calculated and Plato visited,
    invited by
the tyrant to set up his Republic (Dionysius was only
    joking).

Syracuse, New York, once the Lunchpail-by-the-Lake,
    is on the land
of the Onondaga, the Stone Age tribe of Iroquois
    whose name the Europeans
gave the salt lake when it was clean and clear.
    Syracuse in Sicily
was built by Greeks beside a salt marsh they called Sirako.
    So history ramifies
in my native neighborhood, making spurious connections
    to the pealing bells of home.
The principal of Huntington Elementary School was Miss
    Elsie Platto, pronounced *plat-toe*,
homonymous with a feature of geography, not the Greek
    philosopher,
and she was nothing like Borden's cow but slim and trimly
    dressed in tasteful suits.

If you throw a hundred-carat emerald or a golf ball into
    the azure sea lapping
at Siracusa's scenic shore, the ripples kiss the ancient world
    all over its body.

They knew nothing of us, we know nothing of whoever is
 two thousand years
up ahead, and neither of us could have imagined a factory
 on the lake
in central New York named for Ernest Solvay, a Belgian
 chemist who
invented the process for making soda ash, sodium
 carbonate, an alkali
"whose production is sometimes used as an indicator
 of economic health,"
says Wikipedia with anonymous authority. Six kilos
 a year
for every one of us--every man, woman, child on earth--
 to make glass,
soap, detergent, paper, to soften water, scrub flue gas
 from power stations,
"especially where they have to meet stringent emission
 controls."

Did I mention that King Dionysius the Elder of Sicily
 invited Plato to come visit,
work on his tan, set up his Republic (the king was only
 joking).
Archimedes designed his screw, his catapult, his grapple
 for plucking hostile ships
out of the harbor, dropping screaming sailors from the deck
 like rain.
A Roman soldier killed the genius when, so the story's told,
 he wouldn't budge
from working out some numbers in the sand.

The H-bomb followed the A-bomb and we learned to cover
 our eyes and hide
under our desks in Huntington Elementary School where
 Miss Platto reigned.

They drove us to the French Fort and Salt Museum built on
   a low hill by the lake.
Try to imagine, urged the teacher while we looked at rusted
   tools,
the first brave explorers in the wilderness who came all
   the way from France
for salt and to convert the Iroquois and could never have
   imagined
a bus driving us along the lake to visit a museum and
   the replica
of a fort the French explorers never built themselves
   or slept in.

"In inland plants, such as that in Solvay, New York,
   the byproducts
deposited in waste beds have led to water pollution by
   calcium and chlorine
ions substantially increasing the salinity in adjacent
   Onondaga Lake,
among the most polluted lakes in the U.S., a superfund
   site."
For the instant of a recalled afternoon in nineteen fifty-four,
   the two are joined,
the salt city on the ionized lake and its Mediterranean
   sister where
an ancient age's Einstein lay soaking in his bath, calculating
   the sphere
inside the cylinder inside his head, shouting apocryphally
   Eureka!
when the answer came, running dripping wet and naked
   in the street.
Despite his genius Archimedes could not imagine us, or
   a nameless Jesuit
explorer camped beside the lake polluted by the factory
   passing by the bus

driving us to the replica of a stockade fort no one ever
    built or slept in.

Once a year we go for a picnic in the park along the lake
    but no one swims.
Beth and I approach the edge as if it were sulfuric acid;
    we don't put in a toe,
not a finger, we stare at the line where the ripples lap
    the stones
to see what the poison looks like, if there's a stain
    or smell.
Nothing, just the stones, the water lapping, willows
    by the shore,
and all the fish are dead. The French explorers and
    the Iroquois
like everyone who came here came for salt, a pillar
    or barometer
of civilization, like the production and consumption
    of soda ash.
All history is here if you know how to look, the Greeks,
    the Romans,
the Iroquois Nation, French explorers, missionaries, all
    for salt,
for thirteen pounds of sodium carbonate per person per
    year per globe.
It's all here! I'd like to blow it up, the plant, the fort,
    the lake,
the bus, the school, blow it all to smithereens.

The bus grinds gears downshifting as it turns off James
    Street,
named for the grandfather of William and Henry who
    made his money
buying up the land treatied out from under the Onondaga,
    then he flipped it.

Of course I know the French Fort, the Salt Museum, and
   the ionized lake
have nothing to do with the excited physicist rising up
   apocryphally
from his bath with the solution to a puzzle lighting up
   his head
in the most beautiful city the Greeks ever built more than
   two thousand years ago.

The bus is leaning around Sunnycrest Drive past the public
   golf course where
we go sledding when it snows. Syracuse, the Salt City, has
   a quarter million residents,
the kind the Kremlin covets, hard-working, lunch-bucket
   patriots.
The sky is low and gray and if you're blessed to be employed
   by Solvay Process,
Crucible Steel, GE, Carrier, Bristol Labs, New Process Gear,
   Timken Roller Bearing
you do your job, pay your dues, respect the flag. Johnson's
   Supermarket
hands out pamphlets at the door titled "Red Channels" warning
   customers of Stalin's
little helpers, covert Commies disguised as harmless radio and
   television entertainers,
and Siracusa on the sunny island Sicily is run by a secret society
   of thugs.
Archimedes, Dionysius, and Plato are famous ancient names
   and Cicero,
New York, is ten miles north of Syracuse, just past the airport.

The bus has stopped in front of Huntington Elementary School
   and we disembark,
jet-lagged, freed at last from history's cage of lamely welded
   joints.

Today they take the kids to the Erie Canal Museum; the ditch
    was dug across
the state by immigrants, a wonder of the world in eighteen
    twenty-five,
connecting west to east, making Syracuse the hub of New York
    State it used to be.
I walk home under maple trees, past the Murphys, the Rosencrans,
    the Hawks.
The city soon will shrink, ripple back; like Siracusa, Sicily,
    the peak is past.
Ours was a lower peak, no dripping Archimedes shouting
    in the street
apocryphally, no Plato on vacation; just another urban engine,
    rusting now,
the French Fort, the Salt Museum, the filled-in canal, and
    on the Rez
the children of the Iroquois sell tax-free cigarettes. I'd like
    to see a photograph
of what the Roman lawyer saw when he called Sirako
    the greatest Greek city
and the most beautiful of them all two thousand years before
    Beth and I
stood on the shore and wondered what was in the rippling
    sky blue water
no one touched or drank or swam in.

Baby Teeth

You can't describe the twentieth or
twenty-first centuries without using
the word new. Teeth are not new.

Testing them for strontium 90 is new,
a radioactive isotope in fallout from
nuclear bombs or waste from reactors.

Fallout was new when we were kids,
radiation falling out of the sky
from testing nuclear weapons.

We've gotten used to this too.
The tests were halted (that was
the word they always used, halted),

now we get it from reactors melting down,
like Chernobyl's. Melting down is new
too and means the fuel gets so hot it

 liquefies the core and destroys the reactor.
It has also become a figure of speech
like dissolving in tears or going bananas,

which just sounds funny. There's nothing
funny about nuclear fission or strontium 90.
It's a "bone seeker." It collects in the marrow

causing cancer. It also collects in teeth.
The Baby Tooth Survey in 1963 found fifty
times more strontium 90 in baby teeth

than in 1950. They showed us films at
school starring Mister Tooth Decay whose
top hat, tux, and sassy wink became a figure

in our dreams. I lived for Fleers' pink Dubble
Bubble, Chum Gum (three sticks a penny!),
Sky Bar, Snickers, Three Musketeers, and

had more cavities than anyone. Every day
I spent a hoarded nickel on my drug of
choice and if I was short I reached up and

took a coin from Dad's dresser, compounding
sin with crime. Mr. Shanahan's red shiny
face under his paper butcher's hat grimaced

with resentment at the power of money
in his pint-sized customers' sticky hands,
and I resented the power his pink gum had

over me. On the drive to Dr. Colby's office
I took short panicked breaths, rehearsing
pleas for mercy. Outside the car window

the strip of stores, restaurants, parking lots
glided by unstoppably. Could I jump out
and escape the drill? Where would I go?

The long walk up the wide dusty stairs
toward the antiseptic smell led to the waiting
room where Dr. Colby's joke was mounted

on the wall, a shellacked decapitated fish head
with a full set of human choppers. "If it's okay,
raise your right hand. If it hurts raise your left."

I raised my left as soon as he started the drill.
It made a sound like grinding gravel, shot
a flaming wire into my brain, jerked me

in the chair. Dr. Colby called Beth "Whistle
Britches." The nickname made Mom cringe.
Beth was a better person than me, she didn't

chew Dubble Bubble, but she still got drilled,
she jerked and cried. My desire to quit
the daily trips to Shanahan's mocked me in

the dentist's chair. I thought of praying but
didn't trust it to be tested that way. I knew
the next day I'd have another nickel in my

pocket on the way to buy pink gum. Besides
Mister Tooth Decay and warnings not to get
in cars with strangers, we saw movies of

the H-bomb mushroom and bodies stacked
in concentration camps. These were new
pictures too, as new as we were, but we

didn't know they would soon belong to us
the way we owned our teeth. My baby
teeth all fell out by the time I was twelve,

like Mom said they would. I could have quit
chewing bubble gum before the permanent
ones came in but I didn't. I couldn't stop.

Becoming a Parent

They asked me if I would join them,
become one of the parents, make
them three. They were outnumbered,
they needed help. It was meant as

an honor, too, I suppose--isn't adulthood
something we all aspire to?
We want to grow up, we resent
the puny numbers of childhood,

dependence and vulnerability,
we want to get old fast and take
over our life, so of course I said
yes, I'll do it, I'll leave childhood

early, become one of you. It was
an experiment too, in service of
an ideal, treating me like one of
them. What I learned from it most,

I suppose, was the existence of
an ideal, so later when another
appeared I recognized it for
what it was: something other,

unassailable, invisible as a god,
yet it didn't exist unless you
believed in it. That was the lesson,
to implant the embryonic arche-

type in the soft tissue of a child's
mind where it would grow as

he grew, always bigger than him,
a part of him he could never be.

Danny Boy

When his father asked him what he'd named
his second son, Dad said, "We're calling him
Daniel." His father said, "It sounds Irish."

Grandpa was a Baptist minister baptized in
an anti-Catholicism his son had outgrown.
"I found it in the Bible," Dad said he told

his father. But he said it with a tilt and bob
of his head as if it was a neat wisecrack,
and when I laughed and said, "You *did*?"

he smiled but didn't confirm it. I couldn't
imagine him sassing Grandpa. I could make
wisecracks but there was a look in Dad's eyes

I didn't cross. With the others he could be
more like himself but with me he was some-
times his father whether he knew it or not.

The Fat Lady of the Midway

Four hundred and eleven pounds! screamed
the banner hung behind the booth where you
gave your ticket to the turtlefaced man
with the silver-globed microphone growing
out of his cheek beside his cigarette--
he could smoke with no hands! Of all the sideshows,
fireeater, snakehandler, motorcycles driving
around the inside wall of a huge wooden
cylinder, why did Beth and I go in there?
Now Mom was coming in too, as if she
didn't want us to see such a sight untended.

The Fat Lady sat on a short couch, a squinting
toad, feet just touching the raised platform
under her throne. Her dyed yellow hair hung
like wet straw down to the collar of her lime
colored dress. We used the waiver of childhood
to stare at the blobby pyramid of green pleats
set on the sagging cushions but she granted
us nothing, staring back with her own impotent
malice. If she spoke, she was going to say,
    What choo lookin' at?
as if we hadn't just paid for that very right.
But the voice I heard was behind me, genteel
and familiar: "Hello, how do you do? These
are my children." Mom, I nearly said out
loud, you don't talk to them! When I turned
around I saw to my further horror she had
sat down in the single chair facing the freak,
as if she was settling in for a visit.

The Fat Lady didn't respond to the question.

"Are you all right?" Mom asked the silence.
"Do they treat you well?" She wouldn't stop!
She was trying to start a conversation with
the Fat Lady! How could she not understand
the etiquette of the Midway? "My back hurts,"
the Fat Lady said in a small tired voice
that didn't match her angry eyes. "Do they
let you move around?" Mom asked. "I can't
walk by myself," I heard her say as I took
Beth's hand and pulled her toward the exit
hoping Mom would follow. Out through
the canvas flap into the braying amplified
turtlehead voices, the nasal snakecharming
bellydancer music, the revving crepitating
motorcycles driving on the inside of a wall,
as contemptuous of gravity as any other law.
The dense night air was flocked with insects,
the Midway's unnatural wonders glared in
neon, heat, and smoke.

I was still holding Beth's hand, not leading
her now but holding on, stuck in place. After
dutifully touring the Empire State's preening
civic displays, the industrial pavilion's
Nuclear Age of the future, then back to the past
in cow barns and sheep pens, our urban hearts
snagged by bunnies and piglets, their sows
freaks of size too but honored with ribbons
instead of satirical thrones, we had our reward--
the cheap thrills of the Midway. Fair-goers
eating pink bouffes of cotton candy surfed by,
the electronic racetrack flashed and clanged,
turtlehead barkers spun roulette wheels for
packs of cigarettes, they challenged heroes
to win a prize for their pretty girl--shoot

a bullseye, dart a balloon, swing a sledgehammer.
When we reunited with Dad, we'd go on
the rides, the roller coaster, the Jurassic seesaw,
the Ferris wheel with its swooning view of
the Midway, and my favorite, the bumping cars!

But where was Mom? I turned Beth around
and went back into the tent, leaving the noise
behind us again. Mom was still in the chair,
listening to the Fat Lady complain about
sitting there while people stared at her. No,
that's what I was afraid she was saying.
When I tuned my ears to the small tired voice
I heard her describing her feet, how they hurt,
with Mom murmuring Yes, Uh-huh, Oh, really,
I'm sorry to hear that, her sympathy subversive
but not revolutionary. The four hundred plus
pound woman was no longer the freak queen
of the Midway, but a small tired voice with
sore feet and the freakish world was outside
the slit in the canvas flap. Or maybe it was us,
more or less normal voyeurs of the grotesque.

In the supercharged Midway the motorcycles
roared around a wall at right angles to the earth,
but in here some force of inertia had overcome
us all. The trip to see carnival sights at the State Fair
had become the anti-exotic and our whim to see
a monstrosity of fat had become another occasion
when the children are forced to wait--to wait for
the adults to get done with their endlessly dull
conversation so everyone can do something fun.

Query

What would there be
if there were nothing?
I asked Mom, asking again
when she didn't answer.

I don't know. God, I guess.
No, I mean what
if there were nothing.
Not even God.

Well, I don't know if
there can be nothing,
not if there's God.
No! I pleaded, striking each word:

What would *be* there if
there were nothing?
No God, no anything--
What would there be then?

Finally, like God, she ignored me.
I would have ignored me too.
I will die knowing no more
than I did at eight or nine.

Harry Victor White

"Can you do this?" He stood upside
down on his hands, a tall white haired
man, tanned and smiling. Uncle Harry,

Great Uncle Harry, grandmother's
brother from California, who sold cars
and vitamins, was standing on his hands

in the kitchen, as if everyone did, while
Beth and I watched, eyes popping,
speechless--we had no words for this.

When the tall limber old man abruptly
bent down, put his splayed hands on
the floor and flipped his legs straight

up toward the ceiling, his gray pant legs
fell down past his knees revealing
the shiny metal apparatus encasing

both legs, all the way from under
the trousers bunched up at his knees
to the ankles swaying like treetops

below the light fixture. "Polio," said
the voice on the floor. "Pinch me.
Go ahead. Stick a needle in. Can't

feel a thing in either one!" The legs
dropped, the tanned face flipped
back up over our heads and laughed.

Hammer Throw

"Mister Provo throws hammers," the airborne rumor
warned us as we graduated into the bottom grade
    of junior high.
The hammer throw was not a track and field event,
nor a metaphorical one, it was a pedagogical technique
for getting and holding our thirteen year old attention
for a semester of curriculum-required Metal Shop.

Bald as a helmet, drill-instructor lean, strategically
insane Mister Provo was either a good shot or no good at all;
    our uncertainty reinforced his authority.
On the third day, the first week of school, a shout *Look out!*
    clenched the flaccid minutes just before the bell.
Overhead, the tumbling hammer's WHOOSH
    left a comet's tail of awe.
It hit the wall of hanging tools somewhere above Mickey's
head and the *Holy Shit!* expression on his dodging monkey
    face said it for us all.

The crash was like a Koufax fastball thrown through a hall
    of crystal chandeliers.
As a pedagogical technique the hammer throw worked
    spectacularly well.
Metal Shop was loud and quiet.
In a clanging monkish silence we learned to cut, snip, fold,
and bend a sheet of metal to a template, to hammer rivets flat,
to solder seams, and make a scoop for flour to give to mom.

Led by Mickey Kamic, comic prince of insolence,
we left our sabotaging wit and mischief outside the door.
Had we given mom the scoop with the news that Mister Provo
    threw hammers,

she'd have said, "He doesn't really, does he?"
No, he doesn't, really, not if Mickey's never hit.

Times were different then;
a teacher's word had judicial heft,
a pupil's was as light as lies,
and sometimes down the street at
Blessed Sacrament a verbal hammer flew
teaching choir boys how to handle
a clerical erection in monkish silence too.

G-Man

Yeah, that's me in the tux, rented,
and I'd like to be able to say the pose,
the expression on the guy's face was hired too.
But, no, I confess to owning it--having owned it once--
    so proud and ambivalent,
determined to escape from the room the snapshot
    was taken in;
the hassock we rolled around on as kids is under my
    polished black shoe,
a toy peeks out from a corner of the middle class
    playpen for children,
the juice glass in my hand holds water instead of
    usquebaugh--
how can the guy in the tux not know he's a joke?
Maybe he does, so proud and ambivalent.

If I'd been able to be the Grammatical Man
    through and through
the guy in the tux wouldn't have been so cranked,
unable not to carry a couple of contradictory ideas
    at the same time.
All the time.

        2.
"I imply, you infer," Grandmother taught.
A little nod, an unsmiling smile
didn't deny the ferocity in her eye,
her regard for proper grammar as
the King James Version's double, its sacred
    secular double.
"It is important to ee-nun-cee-ate,"
she enunciated, lips drawn back across her teeth.
She grew up on a farm, fed the chickens,

killed the chickens, read her Bible,
learned her Bible, made herself into a lady,
    respecting every syllable.
Not to was uncouth, a moral wrong.
Grammar is the bedrock of the Word.

               3.
I picture a deep, invisible structure,
coalescing in the proteins of a mind,
like growing crystals on a string.
Call it potential plus the verb to form,
as if, to define the wind, I hung up a flag.
By grammatical I mean meaning made
    manifest--
the phrase makes me a little sick
like the dream of eating striped green turtles,
which I only did because I was invited,
a guest, wearing a rented tux.
Lightly cooked amphibious princes exiled from
    Deep Time,
a lovely creamy green, nauseating;
what right have I to pull off its paw
with a fork to observe a rule of grammar?
I want to weep, suck my finger, crawl under the drape,
exit the polite, syntactical necessity.

Potential plus the verb to form has no content,
no sentiment. Cathexis, separation,
the very wettest tears,
laughter floating us away--
ungrammatical necessities.

               4.
Our gift for grammar might be a distant
cognate form or umpteenth cousin of arithmetic,
the need to count, the golden mean, Euclid's axioms.

A manifestation of an underlying order underlying us--
if we could see with different eyes--
if we had a flag to show us the wind
(the way it flutters in our speech)--
this coded grail might be visible
the way butterflies see
in ultraviolet light.

The well-made sentence coherently
distracts with story, myth, fiction,
information, news, puzzle, query.
Its dirty secret is sending thrills
up your bloody spine--heroic tales,
romances starring destiny, fantastic
escapades. A mere enabler,
grammar has no solo life,
it has no zing, grammar
is the dullest thing.

                5.
The rented tux makes me stand and move
    a certain way,
it has that mock distinguishing effect.
Dressed up in proper speech we're all deceived
    deceivers, Trivers says, masquerading one.
The tux is costume and my grammar makes
sometimes specious sense of water, fire, food,
    sex, shelter, mystery, explanation.

Tuxedo Junction

The men are in formal evening wear,
    the women in gowns:
Men? Women? We were kids!
And it was what heaven must feel like.

The band, the ballroom, the rotating mirrored
    glitter ball
sprinkling stars all over the girls from school,
transforming them from classmates into sisters
of Venus--actual living creatures only partially clothed,
rising like flowers from the vase of their gowns!
Their inhaled perfume dissolves in the blood,
    combining chemically
with the row of golden saxophones crooning swing
standards as we dance in a movie starring someone
    we'll be, leaving the molted children behind.

Sally's vertebrae under my fingertips flex
    orthopedically with our steps,
the radiant lines in her blue irises are so close
    she looks startled,
but I'm a shy forest creature too, just as surprised
    to find myself
here in the wild dressed in Fred Astaire's tux.

Oh, now she's laughing, at me, at us, at how
    naked one feels
foxtrotting back and forth across Tuxedo Junction
    in these adult clothes,
giddy with feral desires and a child's hot
    embarrassment.

The ballroom is lined with adults, the chaperones
        on picket duty
back there in the shadows, but I'm getting a very
        different message:
all this is approved! We're supposed to dress up
        in these rented black suits
and Hollywood gowns showing off publicly our
        secondary sexual characteristics!
We're supposed to get this close to a girl, so close
        you both know she's a woman
despite the laughably boyish escort dancing her
        around and around
the star-spangled ballroom as if they were
        the American Dream!

All those shadowy chaperones are back there
        against the wall
to make sure we do this, make sure we show off
        with a straight, smiling face,
so emboldened by their encouragement I wonder
        if this new dispensation
extends to replacing the stray curl of hair in front of
        her ear,
or should I pull the soft hook even closer to show
        I get it, I belong in this tux.
But maybe I've already gone too far--my hand
        is sweated together with hers--
this intimacy must be a secret from the chaperones
        or surely they'd ban it.

The Junior League Ball is a costume party,
a rehearsal for a life we won't lead.
There are no electric guitars in the band--
it's called an orchestra--and no one is
shakin' their butt or gettin' their mojo workin'

and we know it
we know the recorded backbeat better than
the live foxtrot
we've heard all the warnings about what
not to do with our new selves;
the older generation's music,
their gowns and tuxedos, are meant
to show us how much fun
we can have if we join the club of grown-ups
and don't act like children let loose with
alcohol, cars, and sex organs.

Driving, Speed

Driving, speed, motion, escape!
Jump in the car just to go, go
somewhere anywhere nowhere,
cruising the streets of a rusted city,

not finding girls, not finding anything,
hauling around in the limbo of now.
Fox leans out the window to give
someone the finger just for

something to do, something to do.
We drive to New York in my lame
topless Jag, miles from work,
defying our Dads, not telling anyone--

Hey, let's go to the Cape!
Sand, balmy air, scrub pine at dawn,
and the ocean--It's infinite, Fox!
The long haul home trailing chagrin.

Back on the road again, rolling west
in Fox's old Caddy with him and Sally
at sixty, a mile a minute ticked off
by the Caddy's motion and mass.

The conundrum says if you keep
traveling half the distance left
to your goal you'll never get there,
never get there, never get--

We're already here, lolling inside
the high-balling Caddy, faster as

we go wester, suspended in speed.
When we stop we step on an alien

planet, tilting dizzily. Not our terra,
these paint-faded gas pumps
standing by wrinkle-faced stiffs.
We leave their towns in the dust,

eating our dust--did you catch
the blurred name as it slid off
the edge of the windshield?
We're already gone, me and Fox,

Sally dropped off in Colorado,
sharing cash, clothes, Camels,
passing this bottle of Cutty Sark
back and forth once an hour

for our rationed flaming gulp--
are you still with me, you there
in the back seat? Fuck the philos-
ophers, Fox, we're going the last

half of a half to the end! A. Huxley
said the twentieth century's gift
to our quiver of thrills was
speed. Will weightlessness be

the twenty-first's? Why not--fuck
gravity too! The enemy always
is stasis; let's just hover at speed
in the last half of a half to no end.

Unborn

How tilting mad were those twenty years
from adolescence on. I can't pull this thread
without unraveling sanity, and no saving pose,
no trope appears to transfigure my biography.

All the everlasting instants I can't outlive:
What you commit glides into history like
set cement. Thelonious Monk wouldn't
overdub recordings; he said you blow a clam

you got to live with that forever. At least
no children were harmed; the prime victim
was myself, besides the women: one
complicit, nameless, the other without

blame, more than blameless. Riding
in the car--I see the STOP sign, looming
up--and hear a female voice say
the doctor told her what he cauterized

had probably (vastest word in English)
prevented her from getting pregnant
and, he didn't say, saved us all.
Saved us all.

North Wind

She hovers like the cartoon
of the north wind in the old
illustrations, lips puckered and
cheeks puffed out, lines that

curl at the tip for the howl.
Actually, her voice is mild,
tentative, and only I can hear
the terrible need it conveys.

She wants something from me,
she wants something I can't
give. She wants me back inside,
hers utterly again, utterly hers

where she can talk to me
anytime about anything and
I can do nothing but listen.
In the howl and blast of her

need I no longer exist.
I'm deaf, dumb, an embryo.
I'm her breath. This is what
I hear on the telephone.

A Wish

"We should have had another child so one
could stay home with us," Mom said. Her
wish would wrench our world into a shape it
could never assume. The one she wants to
add--let's call her Susie--like a rental for
the drive to the airport, the trips to Florida,
the doctor visits, would have had to be--
let's be honest--limited enough to stay home.
She'd be the one Mom was embarrassed by,
a loving drone with a need for praise and
her own constant wish for a more normal
mind so she could have a family of her own,
a wish expressed simply, longingly and
frequently, making her mother so sad and
guilty she wishes she could wave a wand
and make her youngest daughter normal.

What's my wish? Would I like a mildly
retarded extra sibling to be a caregiver,
to help my nonagenarian parents cope
with what's left of their lives? I think I'd like
to have known I'd end up here so I could
have prepared for it. But then I wouldn't
be here, not exactly here, and wherever
I was I'd wish for one thing to change.

And so on and so forth, said the genie
who invented this little game to amuse
itself, watching all the puppet dominoes
topple, and the rippling sight, the light
clacking sound of the endless row endlessly
falling is the pleasant staccato of discontent,

a train of motion moving nowhere, the mad
nag of regret, irreparable regret, tugging
against the dead weight of what's been done.

At Sixty-Eight

Focus very tightly down.
Cut the rock to the facet showing just this aspect.
What the source of division was.
Division? Cleavage.
It's not a facet,
not just one.
It's jagged, a geode of crystals.

I couldn't relax and inhabit my neighborhood
the way it was, the way I was.
I had to guard it, police it, fix it.
Yet I was just a boy;
why was this big notion in a boy's head?
Why is it there now, scraped with age
but still a jagged shape.

At sixty-eight, an age once considered old
(he might die at any moment)
I still don't know this essential thing.
What was it separating me--
was it the urgency to do something?
But what would do to do?
To feel this force, this hand at my back,
hurrying every minute along
for some purpose I could only sense
as the urgency itself.
There was no actual thing to be done,
it couldn't be imagined.
Not by me.

This is deepest mischief.
To burden a boy who knows nothing

with this chore, this pack,
to load it on again, while he sleeps,
to bear him down like an adult when he's a boy
with some task he can't see or name but only feel,
and to do this--yet, who did it?
Was it an overtone in a progenitor's voice,
a ghost of family legacy? What about
the boy-sized pulpit made for me?
Once I stood behind it mimicking liturgy,
but that wasn't me, that was their son
(what boy needs a pulpit!). The urge
I'm trying to name I found inside my
head without a guide, no key or clue,
the source as masked as the task itself.

I want a scene conjured up, an image,
word, a scent not whiffed before.
Nothing comes; the absent trace
it leaves from need whisks
the task down the road ahead
with a speed that might be like
something out of nothing.
The trace becomes Madame de Stael's
notion of what's out there beyond,
not alien but unlike, transcendent, spacious,
more in a way that cannot be imagined.
Who wouldn't want to go? she asks.

2.

If there was something I had to do,
must not fail to do,
which no one knew,
including me
carving me out from the background
where everyone, it seemed,
was in a different motion--

Maybe it's so simple, that's what it became:
I mean that's it grammatically,
the question posed without the words.
As soon as I decant it into speech
the notion vaporizes.
Let the grammar stand,
the form of question,
the skeleton, the urge to ask,
the thing I had to do to do.

At sixty-eight it's too late,
I shouldn't say a thing.
Shut up,
look wise,
smile.
One must learn
not to understand.

Shameless Thing

It's after dinner.
We're all sitting around the table.
Dad walks in.
"Dear...didn't you forget something?" Mom says.
She laughs, with that screwed up expression of chagrin,
    amusement, wryness of age.
Dad is wearing only his padded shorts.
He just came home from the hospital.
The procedure was successful but the dementia remains.
When he stops by the bathroom door to catch his balance,
    he puddles the floor.
The padded shorts are loose and don't do their job.
Mom gets up to go help him.
We clean up the mess.

The shameless thing was a cleanly bald man, "the baldest
    man I ever saw," in Mark Twain's telling,
who fell overboard in the river, and when he bobbed up
    head first a woman shrieked at the sight of skin:
"You shameless thing--and ladies present! Go back down
    and come up the other way!"
Twain told it as a joke, although it really happened,
    just like that.

The next night we were sitting around the same table.
Dad sat with his head in his hands, tired after dinner but unwilling
    to be unsociable, to go lie down.
Mom said, to illustrate the unsuitability of a man who wanted
    to buy the cottage,
"When he came in to the chorale rehearsal, his sister said,
    'Come over here and fuck me, Jimmy!'"
Mom is ninety-two.

We've never heard her talk like that before.
"Are you shocked?" she said, her question expressing
 a little satisfaction.
"Go back down and come up the other way,"
 I said.

2. Beth

Bald

She sent me a jpeg, a portrait
she took of herself, a close-up
in profile against a white wall
with a sober, inward expression,

the kind your face might assume
at the moment you realized,
internalized, got it right through
your head and into the cells

of your brain that you were
not immortal, that the instant
the shutter snapped was a life-
time. For the camera she was

skinned, newborn, naked to fear,
a sixty-four year old woman
confessing her skulled self.
Then, a second shot: the bald

head has turned ninety degrees
and is staring straight at the lens
with the same unblinking candor
as the first, but now there's her

smile, a sunburst. Not quite
her biggest one, but genuine.
It says, forget the news, this is
me, still me, the real me, Beth.

First Look

She knew my secret (it wasn't a secret)
I was small and wanted to be big,
wished I was Superman to protect her.
She coddled a form of the delusion,

protecting me too. The peculiar look
we could see in the other's eyes, the most
private self, so much knowledge so exposed,
it struck us dumb sometimes, so we kept it

commonsensical, nonsensical, like joking
on the phone the last time when I'd locked
myself out and had to climb in the window
to answer the ringing and she was riding

to the hospital to get an implant of a drug
that wouldn't save her. If we had seen
each other, staring together from the brink
of the end, we'd have seen the faint light

from the first look like astronomers
measuring spacetime by the redshift of
light from a star blinking wetly: This is
your new sister and you must protect

the look in her eyes. It was so new we
could stare into the pre-literate raw
animals we were, see how new we both
were; it made us laugh, our idiot joy.

A Second Look

When I went back to look at
the photos I saw how much memory
had added to my description.
The first shot was just her

letting the camera record her
in profile, knowing her baldness
would be shocking but not looking
shocked herself. Just thoughtful:

this is what is. The second was
closer to what I described, a trusting,
humorous, warm-hearted smile
inviting us to be part of her life.

The contrast between what I
remembered and what's actually
there reminds me the photo was her
and memory can only be my own.

Clairvoyant

I look at the photo of her and me
taken six months ago--she is leaning
into my shoulder, arms linked around
me as if I'm some sort of prize she won--

and I wonder: What if we knew then
it had already found some new part
of her to invade and our happiness
she was cured was hopelessly innocent?

But any teen can see into the future:
we all walk around with some seed of
destruction waiting to bloom, we all
need some sleight of mind to trick us.

Possession

There's a much earlier photograph of
a bassinet on a couch, a little boy in a
striped t-shirt standing on the cushion,

hands on the white wicker edge, smiling
at the newborn baby below. He lost a rib
when she was born but learned he could

sustain his priority if he made the little
girl his own, played her protector, obeyed
the ancient assumptions heaped on his

cameled back: Your life stands for hers,
hero. The warm tingle of praise, jealousy
co-opted by possessiveness--one passion

cancels another (how much did Mom
know?). Now I stand over the hospice bed;
sixty-four years apart, the scenes frame

her life, baby to girl to woman to wife and
mother. I made her mine to hold on to an
eminence; possession possessed us together.

The Meninges

It was the first time I'd heard them talk
in such a tone of voice: grave, hushed,
as if someone shouldn't overhear,
but there was only me, big-eared, scared.
Mom was pausing at the top of the stairs,
not yet going down, Dad behind,
in the darkened doorway to her room.
"Do you think we should take her to
the hospital," she said.
"Let's see what the doctor thinks," he said.
The doctor brought his stout black bag,
bulldog face and medicinal smell.
He left behind a word he said could
paralyze or kill: meningitis.

Six decades later, sixty years almost,
I heard its echo: the meninges.
The malignancy had made another leap
and what leapt in mind solely from the sound
was an archipelago, a chain of rock, scenic
and remote, the home of solitary sea birds--
but no, my ear was wrong. Not geography,
anatomy; the meninges' *dura mater* is the tough
mother wrapped around the spinal chord and
brain where migrant tumor cells now
multiplied in her cerebrospinal fluid.
Somewhere on the globe, in, let's say,
Las Meninges, a remote and scenic chain
of rock, the albatrosses feed their young
plastic trash embossed with fish eggs
so the chicks starve with bellies full
of bottle caps, lighters, and balloons,

far from any hospice.

Thus my disbelieving brain makes crazy
leaps and so does Mom's; she thinks
Do Not Resuscitate means they'll cut
up her daughter for her organs
unless we stop them, now.

The Mole

It fascinated me, large and black,
its furtive name, but soft;
a beauty mark on a private part.
It scared me too; I couldn't understand:
Was such a blatant dot on her nether lip allowed?
"It's just a mole," Mom said, "but we're going to
   have it taken off."
Another Why?
"Because the doctor said it's best."
A third?
"Oh, just in case..."
Of what? What was the threat, the mystery?
The house that never moved felt dizzy.

We were naked kids, ignorant of indifference,
moles in private spots were semi-public mysteries,
a smudge a dirty finger might have left pointing
   at her secret.
What I knew of her and she of me we had no
   language for,
as common to each other as our own edenic skin,
limbs entwined, all but innocent, playing
   mom-and-dad.
She wriggled away restlessly;
there was nothing else to tell.

I don't remember what she looked like with it gone,
so maybe this excision bridged the time between
when we could be together nude and then could not:
"You're getting older now, it's better not."

It bothers me, breaching her privacy,

now she can't describe herself.
Yet it was there, the perfect black imperfection
    on her whiteness,
everything she wasn't compressed into that immense
    tiny dot.
I imagine how, a child, she let the doctor
look at her so trustingly (I knew that look so well),
apologizing for the mole as if some fault was hers--
because it was hers, her private property.
Was it the guiltless sign of some guilt
precursor, the mortal curse, harbinger of
the mutinous lump or lesion
that grew in her breast and brain
more than half a century later?
I shudder; a contaminated thought.

Perhaps, I think like one diseased,
if I replay history now I might change it,
or, unscientifically, that when
they tried to erase the mark
it morphed, went underground
from labium to breast to brain,
not to be denied. Or maybe
it was nothing, really not, just
some random blemish, put there
by chance (but not by accident).
Half a century back we could believe
an omniscient mind willed into being
each spot or dot, hair, feather, pore or cell
of any girl or bird or beast--as if we had
an inkling of the programming force that grows
each mighty one but got it slightly wrong.
Absent information, with only myth and fantasy
to explain it, we imagined something like ourselves
raised to the nth degree, with character and traits:

awareness, jealousy, and most odd of all,
    love.
Now we know for sure melanocytic nevi
and malignant neoplasms have naught
to do with that.

Native Archetype

A classic native archetype: the seven
of us walking up the steps of church,
informally arranged on the ascending
stone blocks: Dad holds the door for Barbie,
Danny, then the eldest, me; Mom in her

Easter hat herds Jonny last, the youngest
of her five. Beth, a little lady, centered, is
the center of our modest, moral universe.
From this half-posed shot one might project
a civilization, fully ordered and filigreed

down to details only God can see. I was
outside, she within, a pair of opposites
except for where the journey up the stone
steps led; the communion cup tastes the same
to both. The little Easter girl, smart blue eyes

radiant, rapt, a vessel brimming with
the Holy Spirit: Do with me what thou wilt,
O Lord, Thy will is mine--that couldn't last.
The inhaled air vaporized the myth and left
a gap between herself and her. Down there,

out there, back there somewhere where it all
mattered so much to her, to me--all those
details only God can see--a pungent residue
condensed. My finger wipes the rim and tastes:
this is who we were together once upon a time.

Seized

The truant mind, streaming away from its host
unconsciously, wordlessly--she chastised herself
for her flaws (much exaggerated), but it's me too;
the family stare, as her husband called it,
takes us all in, the shared petit mal, the seizure
of absence, a hollowed out moment, static and
boundless. As it comes on Mrs. Nichols, leading
us through 5th grade, recedes to the far end of
a very long room, taking her voice with her.
It didn't scare me, not much, I sought it, savored it,
wished I knew how to fall into its trance any time.

Whatever it was neurologically--stray wave
washing over the brain, legacy of
a grandfather's fugitive overnight hike
out of himself--the spontaneous stoned
holidays were tics to be smiled at. Then
a real blow showed deeper down it was serious:
She blacked out and fell with no warning. An
abnormal electrical discharge shorts out
consciousness; you drop into a hole like Alice
in Wonderland (except Alice was there, quite
aware) and the syncope seals itself up with
a strip of amnesia. You return from far, far
away on the floor, in a chair, in the street.
But not on your feet. She fell the first time in
a balsa wood, rice paper house on the other
side of the globe and came back, a new mom with
a babe in her arms. Childhood meningitis plus
stress of pregnancy equaled grand mal epilepsy.

In the quavery voice Mom dropped into to speak

of taboo, so dissonant with the formal *your sister*,
she said: "Your sister has something to tell you.
She wants to tell you herself." "They can treat it,
there are drugs," Beth assured me, but we both
heard gongs in the background: Dad's own epileptic,
brain-damaged sister, a subject, a fact, a person
at times taboo, at others an object of familial
Christian love: Suffer the least of these to come
to me. Now Beth was one of the least, her
infirmity making Mom speak in that seized
quavering voice, and the young mother needed
help besides drugs, a special doctor to treat
an ill of the brain spread to the mind, awakening
ghosts. She learned to negotiate helplessness,
its dizzying fear, it's cunning doubling denial:
Your brain can't be trusted. Who says? I do.

It's all in my head! I hear her joke now, trying
to make a deal with her brain. She wondered,
at certain solo moments, about her peculiar
cerebral history, the smartest kid in her class,
the abnormal flashes of darkness, the mirror
neurons that some said were wellsprings of
empathy, of putting yourself in someone else's
shoes, imagining yourself an Asian, for instance.
This time the metastasized cells were nestled
together in the helmeted squishy tissue along
with the calming rational ones for assembling
jigsaw puzzles and conjugating French endings
on Japanese verbs. The organ defining her most
had contained an abyss, now it could kill her:
mind under matter, mind undermined.

Betrayal

It must have made us even closer, the way
she was her father's daughter, born to get
along in the best of all possible worlds
(not ideal just the best evolution could do)

and I was hatched from Mom's ambivalent
egg, thrawn, contrary, secretly going one's
own hard way, a tiny pair of Hell's Angels'
wings fluttering deep in her warm heart, in

mine. There are so many ways to hurt people,
like Rogers in gold rush Arizona hung by his
heels over a slow fire, or Mom deciding Beth
wasn't really her daughter and telling her so.

They might have just shot Rogers if his crime
had been murder or theft, but betrayal--
leaving them out in the desert to go crazy
with thirst--so they opted to heat up his brain

and watch it run out his ears. Beth married
outside the tribe, became so Japanese she mated
with one of its sons. If she could do that,
she must not be my daughter, thought Mom.

It was a fantasy, but felt like discovering
a hidden truth, and when she arranged other
facts around it to see how everything fit, it fit
like one of Beth's jigsaw puzzles. We were

right there in the kitchen, about to go out for
a walk, when Mom began describing how

the doctor switched babies at the hospital.
Her voice had an implausible soap opera

plausibility, but hearing it, Beth saw another
truth: If she'd been reborn in Japan then she
really wasn't her mother's daughter, not the
way she had been before and, standing there,

mute, with her husband beside her, she couldn't
deny she was an impostor. Besides that, she
realized, she had also broken a rule of self-
preservation: For loving her mother defense-

lessly she now had to suffer the diabolical
yin the yang of her goodness aroused. It had
happened before, in kindergarten when
Miss Baker made her cry because she was

perfect and defenseless, and perfection and
defenselessness were affronts to reality,
properly punished by demanding Beth obey
contradictory commands about how to eat

cookies and milk. In eleventh grade, hunch-
backed Miss Durkin, imprisoned in unwed
History, bullied her compliant pupil to tears.
The reward for virtue was envy, she learned.

To make her feel better now I said, "Ignore what
Mom says, she *acts* as if you're her daughter."
Hung up by her heels, her brain running out
her ears, Beth couldn't hear, didn't care what

I said. She shook off her husband's comforting
hand and strode tearfully under the palm trees,

past the rows of immobilized mobile homes.
Cancer was merely bad luck--nature had nothing

against her, except maybe for loving too much--
but she knew hate when she felt it and we
couldn't protect her. When Beth died did Mom
behave as if she'd lost her own child? She seemed

worn, disoriented--was it the lack of a church
service, as there should have been for her child?
To compensate, or retaliate, Mom read the
Twenty-third Psalm aloud to all of us.

Her voice quavered with anger as much as
grief; anger at change, at the daughter she lost
to Japan, now to death, at the loss of her place
in her world, the loss of her world. Listening

to the psalm's blessings, its promised protections,
I saw Beth, dis-mothered, her head ringing with
pain, beside a gold digger hung by his heels
over a slow fire, his brain running out his ears.

Rhymes With

The rhyme with her name is so obvious
but I only hear it here where it feels like
a coincidence, chance, a false lead.
The suffix -eth is archaic yet bespeaketh
tradition which she respected, so it's apt,
but the leaden D hints at doom and dread
(I see her shaking her head--not her style
or size) while her own B suggests blessed
and brimming: her smile reappears in beatitude.
There's no way to marry her to the Reaper,
to make her fey, foreordained for demise.

Instead of eschatological, her disposition
was upbeat and sunny, spreading cheer
with a wink of irony, a self-mocking quip
smuggled in before you could say,
"You can't really be *that* cheerful!"
She wasn't. It was her duty to smile
--if she wouldn't do it, who would?--
yet it wreathed an astute critic's eye,
soothed a toothache of the heart,
and led the embassy of her private mission:
hopeful, urgent, a nudge in the back,
at times almost evangelical,
to celebrate the best of what is
and what might be no matter what.

Deeper down, beneath the smile, smoldered
fear: of might, force, thumps in the night.
The smile beseeched mercy, a wary trust
in civility and law to stave the brute.
Men are bad, everyone knows, but

can be made better; disease is worse:
deaf, unconscienced, no mind of its own
to train or entreat. "I'm not brave,"
she warned her doctors, who listened
and nodded, squeezing her hand,
though they could not stop what
was squeezing her brain.

"Why do I need to rhyme with anything?
I thought that went out a long time ago,"
she laughs. "Breath, if you insist, but
don't hang any precious words around
my neck. Just call me the Sleep Champ."
Her drug of choice was a snooze, yet
despite the appeal of unconsciousness
what I hear in her short, quick name,
besides the wee voice of our childhood,
is a grin, a hug, a jest, a wish--anything
but dirge, threnody, requiem, taps.

It would be out of character for her to die,
too busy thinking of others. Sitting on
the edge of the hospice bed beside Barb,
no longer able to speak, she buttoned up
her younger sister's jacket the way she did
when they were kids, just trying to help.

Chadao

"Mamakodama" is who she became,
the finished self, wife and mother:
Neat, rhyming, witty, her email
handle winks when you say it.

Her children are her works of art,
expressions of her sense of beauty,
humor, morality, sociability. Her
two works bestow their grace

on each hallowed being, each
cousin in the Whitmanesque family
of man. Her own delicacy of manner
treats each biped with tea ceremony

respect as if the spirit of an ancient
rite might tame the rogue, shame the bully,
ignite the conscience latent in the thug
and lubricate the chafing friction so

everyone would brightly, newly see and
feel the common pulse. Each is special,
to themselves at least, and might some-
how adopt their own sublime chadao,

the way of tea. Mama knows they won't
but hopes and hopes, and jokes to hide
the hurt: our mortal flaws the way of
tea must also venerate without excuse.

Hurricane Brain

She named it in her CarePages blog, how it came on in a rush,
    almost as fast as she could type,
transcribing the thoughts spewing out after they Gamma
    Knifed ten tumors
in one session and gave her a whopping dose of Decadron
    to prevent swelling.
Jeffrey met a guy at Dana Farber on Decadron who went down
    to the cellar
in the middle of the night to pound nails in a 4x4 post trying
    to burn off the steroid;
Beth sat down at her computer and plugged herself into
    her readers.
The torrent was coherent and grammatical, channelled by
    practice,
inspired by all the clichés, the inescapable endgame clichés,
    that now described her.

She had a friend who'd fought depression her entire life;
then she got the dreaded disease and was told she might,
    at the max, live a year.
Like magic her mental illness was cured.
All this would soon be over; she could relax, free of an anguish
    more tormenting than death:
the year she spent dying was the best year of her life.

Beth's anguish was different. A good marriage, a career, two
    beautiful children, two beautiful grandchildren--
a cheerful, witty middle-class woman protected from the grim,
    violent world--
but why was she writing all those notes to nowhere, to no one,
    unmoored from the spirit:
What spirit--the old Holy Ghost?

When she went back over those pages where she'd dumped out
   her mind
she found strange words like God and prayer and even Jesus.

Years ago as an experiment she had gone back to the place where
   those strange words were spoken.
Once or twice, briefly, a signal came through, then fainted
   away.
She was no longer a child who could glow in the pledged
   halie speirit.
Now, trying to dig herself out from under the fresh, unthinkable
   fact--
Your cancer is back: It's in your brain--she typed compulsively,
   unstoppably, a meth-mad stenographer
keeping up with a riot of voices, trying to hear them, record them,
   forever.

In the eye of the hurricane she found the calming power of
   the Word: this word was her own
and fulfillment came from the others: crying out, calling back
   through the ether, cyberspace:
I know just how you feel, you say it so well, so clearly, so
   eloquently, that's just what it's like
and I can't tell you how much it means to read your thoughtful,
   perceptive, courageous words.
What began as an account of the journey she'd been
   abducted upon
became her art form. Steering Decadron's side effect back
   through her brain,
recycling her fear, winding it around the lethal tumors,
   the soul or essence
the Holy Spirit was meant to save had been--not saved at all
   but spent, expended,
thrown out the window like a fistful of million dollar bills
   become a hail of blessings;

and the people outside in the street who found them were
 lighthearted with joy,
swooning, smiling, bowing their heads, partaking of her
 state of grace
while she sat at her keyboard and typed.

Twenty-third Psalm

If the Lord is my shepherd, what is
His flock of sheep doing in my mouth?
she said, laughing.

Steroids made her mouth feel as if
it was full of wool and that's how
she sounded, woolly, except when

she was laughing. If the Lord is
my shepherd why do we repeat this
woolly psalm, solemnly mocking what

He can't do? When mockery fails,
the absurd gives comfort; to mock
is human, the absurd divine.

An Unwarranted Sense of Well-Being

It sounds rather Zen, the punchline to a joke anyone
can fill in themselves, with just that timbre of irony
she often used. In fact--and I should stick to facts,

especially when speaking about an illusion--it said
on the prescription "an unwarranted sense of well-being"
was a symptom for Decadron users to look out for,

even cause for calling your doctor, pretty funny to read
if you were being treated for brain cancer. When she
moved to Eugene, Beth noticed the view of distant

mountains from her bedroom window; in certain light
it looked like a Japanese rice paper print and made
her feel an unwarranted sense of well-being, the same

sensation she often felt during tea ceremony. When
you were preparing for your trip to Provence, I reminded
her (although the nurse said she probably couldn't hear),

you practiced by conjugating French endings on Japanese
verbs. Combining the world's refined babel into one
language was right in character. Granted, only she could

understand the Gallic-Nipponese verbs, but who else
will keep the race's language, civilize us, scold merchants
for putting up Christmas decorations before Thanksgiving

because it upsets our sense of well-being? Her fragile
chest heaves with each breath; the nurse says it's
dyspnea: when your body senses the end, it releases

pain-killing chemicals. The nurse's eyes blink sincerely;

she is sure Beth feels a sense of well-being, and unlike
the steroid's gratuitous effect, nature's anesthesia is

its own warrant. There is no need to call a doctor.
In a properly performed tea ceremony, after the last
bowl has been drunk and wiped clean, the tea scoop,

the whisk and the caddy are admired by the guests,
who are then bowed out the door by their host.

Unwritten Story

My own storm, Hurricane Beth, is not as torrential as hers
but my hand moves with it's own compulsion. I make new
discoveries about her, and us, there is more to say, to ask.

In her last email she said after her treatment was over
she was going to keep writing even when there was nothing
left to say; she didn't know what, maybe memoirs,

not her own but others'--she might help people organize
and edit. She savored how it felt in her brain assembling
puzzles, the sensation even richer using human event,

emotion, syntax, speech instead of abstract shapes. I told
her she should write about a girl, a nice middle class American
girl who went to Japan and found a wholly unexpected new

self who became the center of a wholly unexpected new world
(yet at its center as ever was the need to love, to be loved).
She didn't answer, there wasn't time. I can't write her story

in her stead. I wasn't there, I don't know the land people
language culture. I can imagine the shock of a young
provincial Yankee girl discovering people who were

a different race but just like you, the private you. The young
provincial girl stands exposed in front of the surprise mirror,
the epicanthic fold enfolding her in recognition. The notion

of just who can be just like you expands, ideas fly away,
unreify, what's left is human stuff, refined. I can picture that.
What I can't imagine is her Jane Austen eye enfolding several

thousand graded shades of visage, voice, gesture, nuance, shift.
Plus the exotic scenes and props. Tea ceremony, for instance,
an ancient timeless pantomime instantly familiar, fresh, hers,

a ritual enactment of esthetics, an ordered realm outside
the drab, sordid, sloppy unintended one. The way the tea
is poured precisely signifies, transcending ugliness and lies.

Japan had been created to delight her, to give her soul its
own home. When I tell her this she nods and laughs at
the image of herself as changeling, mysteriously swapped

and swaddled in her small Caucasian figure. The image
shimmers back from the coin flashing on the surface of her
cup of tea as she brings it to her lips to sip. Mom was right,

Beth was not her daughter, and the teasing friend who tried
to bring her down to earth was wrong: "You've got to face it,
Beth--you're never going to be Japanese." She always was.

Twins

The view of Keuka Lake from the cottage porch,
waves lapping on the slate-pebbled beach, and
the Sunday school portrait of Jesus, wavy brown
hair down to his shoulders, a pale yellow light
haloing the Hollywood face--these images had
warmed the members of our sect of just two.

The few precious weeks every summer at
Grandmother's cottage were ordinary perfect
happiness, skipping like Jack and Jill across
the wooden footbridge to Mrs. Porter's, drawn
by the aroma of baking to lick the spoons and
bowls she'd used to mix batter and icing.
Mrs. Porter loved us, and so did Jesus, this we
knew, and we asked to be forgiven for the things
which we ought not to have done as well as
the things undone which we ought to have done.

One day we would sit together on the maroon-
cushioned pew in the cool glow of an absence,
the thirteen billion year old radiation ringing
the universe like another halo. The form in our
paired mind was impossible, the thing undone
would never be done, not by anyone, but anyone
could be chosen to enjoy a special awareness,
a peculiar heightened awareness of incompletion.
If she couldn't be perfect she could always make
you feel better about yourself and with that last
phone call she was doing it again, even while
she was bouncing down the steep front lawn
in the wheel chair--"Don't let go, Ken!" laughing
through the garbled syllabobbles, "I've got a flock

of sheep in my mouth!" Matt was driving
the loveboat ("You're in good form today, Mom"),
to the Clinic of Last Resort, Ken beside her, with
Barb and Emi driving behind, all of them inside
the hurtling Juggernaut, the out of control
virtual vehicle they'd been riding in ever
since the first verdict, and now she was still
trying to make me feel better about life,
not to blame it for being a bummer because
of what it had done to her: Okay, the first time
you went after my breast but that was something
I didn't need anymore so this time you went for
my brain, she wrote in her mock tough-guy
voice, always a self-conscious joke since
the last thing she was was tough, or a guy.
Had she been I wouldn't have felt the same
buzz. We flattered each other as a boy and
a girl, there was always a little of that Adam
and Eve between us, the other's original and
ideal, almost unaware, practicing jitterbugging
to "Come Go With Me" on the back porch.

We were twinned in the glow of a departed
spirit of childhood, now a departing adult one.
After the tears, she faced the end of her turn
as a human like one of those clear-eyed Greeks
sitting on his own cottage porch listening to
the soft lapping waves: You give what you can,
you celebrate joyously, but don't go overboard
praising the flawed terrestrial trip since any
bozo can see how much better it could be.
Don't credit death too much either--
what's the big deal about genetic
signals crossing, rogue cells multiplying,
some organ wearing out.

So hold something back in reserve.
What we imagine is held in reserve.

"I've always felt you were there for me,"
she said, leaving nothing unsaid before
she left, rounding our time together with
the assurance I had fulfilled my first duty,
despite whatever else might have failed her.
One's turn in the sun might be this or that
but as a springboard to love had no critic.
"What thou lovest well remains," Pound
pronounced, as if love could sanctify,
petrify, as if it was a cryogen instead of
something warm and entropic. "What thou
lovest well goes," is more like it, but
we repeat what Ezra said in the hope that
maybe once when we say it, it will be true.
It will be true.

Last Day

Ken spends two hours with her alone saying goodbye.

Some friends play ukuleles and sing "I'll Fly Away."

She lies very still and moves, barely, an eyebrow.

We hold her warm, thin hands and touch her face.

Her narrow chest bellows up and down in a slow rhythm,
as if her spirit is waiting for the right moment to escape.

Emi sings "Maunaloa" in a pure soprano voice.

Matt reads from E. B. White.

Dan plays "Ashoken Farewell" on a borrowed violin.

Barb reads "Lake Isle of Innisfree."

No one says Jesus' name and the next day no one says
Beth is in heaven.

We walk among the gigantic Douglas fir trees in the park
behind the hospital.

Sitting on a bench in the grove of trees, Dad says, "I guess
it's like the Bible says, 'There's a time to live and a time--'"

He is unable to finish.

The Puakenikeni Tree

The Celebration of Life was all improvised.
That was the way she wanted it.
People gathered, told stories,
sang, wept and laughed.

There was no ceremony or funeral rite.
We have outgrown priests and pastors;
they have no magic and our own prose
will do for this occasion.

Each expressed an aspect of what she was:
love humor decency grace conscience joy.
These are just words and now she is a name.

A few months later her in-laws planted
a puakenikeni tree at the Honolulu Zoo.
It's in "an open area framed by large trees,
near a rainforest aviary and the plaque with
her name faces east to catch the morning sun."

Gaudy birds noisy at dawn
in the rising sun
a name beside a tree.

Elephantine

If you are ninety and your daughter dies, what is the quality
of your sadness?

I need to be done with this subject but the quality of my own
sadness makes me feel as if there is something yet to do,

a final ceremony or event to comprehend who she was and
what she meant--not the gathering to celebrate her, which

was lovely but could not conceal the estrangement of loss,
how much we're like a herd of sniffing elephants nudging

the fallen one with their trunks. No, I mean something else,
a medium she might reappear in, idealized but quite natural,

and all us siblings our most natural selves too, meeting for
a final wise, witty, laughing taste of being one of us.

Even if we could do it, I could barely look her in the eyes.
The elephants don't either. There's some animal resistance

to the head-on stare, boggling at two tiny dots of black in
the mirroring face. In such a naked look we might see our

family secret, our shared consciousness of self, the elephantine
mystery, and now the anti-climax, that it should come to this.

No cadenza, no finale, no consummation, only this. Sadness is
so small, so little room in these three or four cramped dimensions.

The person gone occupies a geometry not limited by what sense
perceives. If you're old you must feel it doubly, trebly; the child

gone prematurely may be like your youth, lost in history yet enlarged, ghosting the narrow parapet we shuffle on.

Purgatory Fantasy

They got it right, whoever came up with
the concept of heaven's vestibule,
a place the newly dead soul waits while
the ones left behind pray it into Paradise.

I mean the human part, not the medieval scenario.
The period of purification (she wouldn't need that)
is also the time of most intense mourning,
a salving theological construct and
the real mental hell of those left behind.

She's already out. She flew away.
I know it because Jane saw her in a dream;
she was happy and laughing.
I can hear the laugh,
a little strained as it sometimes was,
as if she was putting some effort into it,
making the occasion a little more happy than it was.
Typical. Giving more than she took,
wanting her laugh to ignite ours,
light us up, make things merry.
The meliorist, advancing the race.

I can't say I'm out yet myself.
We might not be exactly in sync on this.
Yesterday, walking Jingle up the road
on one of those spectacular fall days
the leafers pray for, I felt the kind of joy
she told us to savor after she was gone.
Enjoy joy! I tried to shout. What I feel now,
out from under the spectacular leaves,
is the lameness of trying, of posing for joy.

I could go back and change the repetition--
too many joys--but what the hell.
It illustrates how things can't be undone
and even standing at the edge of the pit
anyone swayed by a strong emotion
is only a membrane away from comic tears,
behaving as if the commonplace was unique
solely because it happened to him, holy him.

Beth's appearing in Jane's dream
means nothing either, I know that,
but we need these little fictions,
throwbacks to a child's fancy,
and that's what I shared with her most,
being children together, and with her exit
she took away all the unspoken things
only we knew, childhood's phantom limb.
One of the things we knew in those missing
days was that this couldn't happen to us.

Wondering

I'm wondering how Beth would feel about my writing
    about her.
Writing about my feelings about her, that's probably okay,
but presuming to get inside her head, to say what she thought
    or felt when how could I know?
She wouldn't like that at all.
It would be intrusive, presumptuous, a form of bullying, even,
    an older brother taking advantage.

It's what writing is about, supposedly,
getting inside someone else,
probing into their deepest feelings,
into things they don't even know about themselves.
Yet everyone knows—it's a commonplace of our time—
you really can't know anyone but yourself and
that's the person you're probably most deceived about.
So where does that leave the conversation?
With its own tail in its mouth, I'd say.

So, can I write about her or not?
Who do I ask, since I can't ask her.
What would the answer be, if I could?
It wouldn't be yes; but it probably wouldn't be no, either.
Like so many important discussions,
we'd talk about it without coming to a conclusion.
Instead, we'd have a sense of the other's feelings about
    the subject.

Right now I'm seeing her face and she looks very
    thoughtful.
"I'm not sure I'd want to read what you wrote about me."
She pauses.

"Maybe I would."
She laughs.
"You know what?—Use your own judgment. I won't
   be here anyway. So of course I won't care."
We look at each other.

This is the moment I was trying to avoid.
The whole thing isn't about personal secrets or breaches of
privacy or opinions about her I never expressed.
It's something else.
It's that look.
That knowledge we have of each other that goes back to
childhood, what it knows about being children of two specific
parents, their culture, the way their genes combined to make us,
and now that we're here the elephantine oddness of life,
of knowing we're here,
that our awareness of being here is
so uncannily doubled in that other person—
a girl, not a boy, blue eyes not brown—
yet with some identical stamp or mark in what the dilated pupil
   perceives.
The puzzle of life, that we're here, is so odd,
it's so odd that we can love so devoutly and it makes everything
odd or doubtful irrelevant, just blows it away—
yet the oddness persists, it's always there,
a descant above the symphony of emotion,
always there, always there,
mocking us even when it sings.

I guess that's what I was asking.
Can I mention that, Beth?—
can I mention what a daydream this has always been compared
to something I can't describe but I know you know too.
Only now I know it alone.

3. Outside World

The Perfect Tomato

There is no perfect tomato.
The market tomato is bred not
for taste but for travel: hard, round,

and unblemished, skin taut like
Spandex, it resists bruising and
rides like a Teamster. It's picked

before it shows pink and blushes
red when given a blast of ethylene
gas to get ready for sale. The heirloom

tomato is bred for taste; soft, lumpy,
misshapen, just picking it up your
finger can puncture its skin.

The meat is not pulpy, the juice isn't sour;
when you taste one your lips smack and
you say, "This is why we grow tomatoes."

Nostalgia

What you once despised
now you love
the memory of
because it was yours.

That's all it takes
to transform the banal
the trite even the agonizing
into something warm

funny achingly cherished;
the haloed days
you pissed away gone.

Twig

I was raking leaves.
They were tracking a deer
shot, the guy said, yesterday.
There was a trail of blood, then just drops,
then nothing, over there at the edge of the woods
in my neighbor's yard.

I didn't know it was deer season yet, I said.
Bow season, he said.
His face was wide open, sweet, penitent.
It had come swimming up into my vision
    while I was raking.
My uncle hunted deer with a bow, I said,
    when it got too easy for him with a gun.
I love it, bow hunting, he said.
You have to be pretty close to shoot with a bow,
    don't you? I said.
Thirty yards. But anything can deflect it.
    A twig.
His son, young, a teenager, was across the road
    by the edge of the woods, looking.
If we don't find him, the coyotes will get him,
    the hunter said.
That's what happens, I said, the coyotes get them?
He nodded, the wide eyes in his sweet face weren't
    exactly aligned, a slight strabismus.
Would that too deflect an arrow, I didn't ask.
Should I call someone if I see it? I said.
He looked around.
Call me, he said, discovering the cell phone in his hand.
I went into the house for a pen and piece of paper.

Later, still raking, I noticed the guy again,
him and his son, walking along the road,
heads down, no longer looking, but still looking.

It snowed the next morning, November's first snow,
not enough to cover a deer, a carcass.
It had stood or lain somewhere waiting,
using its hooves against the coyotes,
being eaten without nurses or morphine
before the lungs slowed, stopped.
Or maybe it was a flesh wound,
a tear in the tight brown coat
clotting, sealing up on its own,
saved by a twig.

Grammatical Incident

"Perhaps ten thousand men from both armies
    fell around it,
three-fourths of them French," said the biography
    of Wellington.
But the description of battle at Waterloo was too
    grammatical
to express what it said.

I had to scramble it into a babel of shouts, cries,
    curses, screams,
grunts, moans, gunshots, explosions, swords clanging
    swords and steel rifle barrels,
bones and skulls cracking, eviscerated whinnying horses,
    guts, blood,
and mud mixed up with severed hands, feet, teeth, eyes,
    balls and intestines.
And even then the exchange between the mounted
    field marshal
and his mounted officer when a ball passed through
    the latter's knee
was way more grammatical than what it said: "By God, sir--
    I've lost my leg!"
"By God, sir--so you have!" replied Wellington.

Dashing Andy

The story of how dashing Andy Jackson
scraped the South clean of Injuns making
space for Big Cotton, savior crop of slavery,
engine of wealth in the English-speaking

world--that tragic epic would read about
the same if the cast of millions swapped skins;
if Andy and his cohort had been red or black,
the victims white, the crime would not have

changed. But he wasn't. He was my racial
antecedent, the first "man of the people"
elected to his democratic eminence. Our
American History loves, mythologizes him.

We confess our crimes in court,
if at all, our sins in church, if at all.
Dashing Andy rides bronzed and horsed,
the victims of his glory dirt.

Wildlife Porn

Attenborough's awed hushed voice is the sound
you'd make disclosing the very deepest secret
of existence to one you loved, a child, perhaps.

His words seem to warm your ear: This is
the miracle of nature, he confides, and it's
never been so gorgeous, so Kodachromatically
seductive to the eye and heart: a polar cub
with cotton-candy Mom, the leopard's lick
in greeting, a goofy panda munching bamboo
like a licorice stick, the loyal waddling
penguin we call emperor, a synchronized
duet of yin-yang orcas: charismatic stars
of the unmanned planet's undirected show.

The majestic sweep of time and season slows
down, speeds up, to display what unaided we
can't see moving through, surrounding us.
The wild living things recorded by the silicon
empowered camera's eye, deftly edited in
swooning sequence underscored with music
and by David's awed hushed voice floating
over all, are like the glossy airbrushed, silicone-
titted babes in Playboy magazine. The volup-
tuous screen star Nature melts to mate Herself
with us, to be our valentine, to hear us sigh
and gasp. We obey her call, staring at her
body parts as she performs the tooth and
claw burlesque we call Survival of the Fittest.

The raw live world is rendered less as earthy
battle than a tease. The captured highlights of

the wild give *Homo sapiens* a voyeur's pleasure,
promising sensations we can't have. Like sex
for the impotent and sterile, beyond the tease
there is no act, no consummation. Well, so what?
Where's the harm? It's only pretty pictures of
the great outdoors arranged to entertain.

2.

Halfway between wild and tame, the Greenland
sled dogs live outside in snow at 25 below,
pull for for five years or so, and then are shot
by the Danish military patrollers who love and
live with them. They can't be pets; there is no
other place for them but working in the cold.

The Greenland sled dogs aren't starring in
this movie. Their story's of another kind:
classic Greek or mythical, sacrificial creatures
doomed tearlessly by fate, by man playing fate.

3.

Also not filmed for this production is
the Great Pacific Garbage Patch, several
thousand square miles of ocean filled with
pelagic plastic beads too small to be seen
by eye, broken down by sunlight and brine
from the tons of trash swept up by counter-
clockwise currents of the North Pacific Gyre.
On the islets of sunwashed archipelagoes,
seabird carcasses lie like *objets d'art*,
their skeletons framing desiccated guts
crammed with bottle caps and other homely
polymers in picturesque designs.
The ecotours don't visit here but halfway
down the globe disgorge awed ironic tourists
on Galapagos to visit evolution's peep

show. From the hotel deck they can see
what Darwin saw, where he rode the tortoises
and snared his finches; they take only pictures
and leave only carbon footprints.

                    4.

One could write an epic about how we,
beginning as a natural consequence, split off
from the Mother Trunk some age ago and have
made ourselves into rivals for our home's
stingy resources, crowding many others
out. Our fecundity is stronger than our
wisdom, a tame faculty insufficient to our
plight, most puissant in regret. And yet, as
super cynic Sam conceded, we must go on.

Someone with a telescope said all of us on
planet Earth are only one supernova or
record-breaking coronal mass ejection or
some other colorful event away from vapor.
In that larger view, the awed hushed voice
and luscious scenes of cubs, leopards, pandas,
penguins, and cavorting orcas aren't porn,
they're home movies. Instead of lewd desire
their esthetically ideal animated images
stand for hope--for Superman or Mighty
Mouse or God, for some being to undisturb
the universe and guarantee our home,
and kindly not crush us under something
else's footprint, or our own.

Glock

An ugly sound--
a tongue-snapping click
back in the throat: GLOCK!
Got you right between the eyes!

German for BANG BANG!
GLOCK GLOCK you're dead, you've been glocked!
Hobnails, goose-steps, chancellors of iron
and blood, a triumph of the will.
The purpose of a gun is to change things now.

A quotation in the newspaper
says we have a God-given right
to carry a Glock.
Thou shalt not go unarmed!
It's not in the Bible,
not one of the big Ten Commandments
(but it could be!);
he must mean the Holy Grail,
the Second Amendment, dictated by
the Lord God Almighty through our
Founding Fathers, bless their hearts.

Tocqueville noticed our American impulse
to do things ourselves, to play the roles
of authority instead of yielding to hierarchs.
In New England town halls the people
are government, no king's ministers need apply.

In our fondest myth the common man was
shipped to America to escape lords and masters,
to escape a feudal history yoking him in iron

to the bloody present. Ever since ever
he hadn't owned his own life;
no one will take it away again ever;
tread on me and I'll glock you!

In our comic book land the pious go armed
the aggrieved, the outraged, the insane go armed.
We take things into our own two hands,
we pull a trigger,
we blow the present inside bloody out
GLOCK! GLOCK!
Did I miss?
GLOCK! GLOCK!
Gotcha that time.

Micicide

Robert Burns did it first famously, turning
the wee sleekit thing up with his plow.
He was guilty yet innocent hoping
the panicked mousie survived. The two
I starved by neglect, white siblings in a box,
I left too long without food or water, unable
to face the fact till they were way past suffering.
The worst act of my childhood, almost.

Last night the weak-springed, too-handy trap
I set only caught the big-eared gray mouse
by the nose; he dragged it off the counter top,
fell on the floor wedged between cupboard
and fridge where he worked his legs for
the next eight or nine hours in the dark
trying to breath through a crushed nose.

I found him at 6:00 A.M., took him outside
and released him. He lay on the ground,
legs working, unable to walk, legs working,
legs working. I picked him up by the tail and
swung his head against a rock. I swung until
his legs stopped working, until I felt sick.

Dzhokhar Tsarnaev's confession was an
homage to his deity sandwiched around
acknowledgement that he felt the burden
of what he had done to the people he hurt
or killed bombing the Marathon. Yet Allah
never gives you a burden too heavy to bear
he assured the court, a pledge to himself too.
Dzhokhar was thinking of Allah, I was thinking

of mice. I wanted to ask--when you saw
what you'd done to your victims, did you
feel sick? Could Allah prevent even that?

The Strad

It was a gift from the Third Reich to a girl,
a daughter of Japan, the Axis' Asian ally,
a particularly gifted sixteen year old who
could make the wooden instrument--
the aged spruce and maple, the varnish,
cat gut and horse hair--sing the most
revered compositions of the genii of
German music's golden age.

The gift had no known provenance,
none but the slender knotted hand
of smiling donor Joseph Goebbels,
Minister of Public Enlightenment and
Propaganda, who had the power to
conjure angelic instruments out of air.

It's into air that the prior owner of
the Strad has vanished. No one knows
today to whom the orphaned violin
might be rightfully returned. Any one
of several million could make a claim.

Trinity

A test-bomb site in the desert called by
the name of the triune God of Christians:
Did Oppenheimer mean U-235, U-238,
and plutonium were standing in
for Father, Son, and Holy Ghost?

"Why I chose the name is not clear,"
Oppie said, and quoted John Donne:
    As West and East
    In all flatt Maps--and I am one--are one,
    So death doth touch Resurrection.
"That still does not make a Trinity," Oppie
conceded, reciting Donne again:
    Batter my heart, three-person'd God
before retreating with a sigh:
    "Beyond this, I have no clues whatever."

The Bomb's battered baptizer and midwife fled
    to the Unconscious for an answer,
into the shade crowded with dreamers and artists
    and quacks of the twentieth century,
a few philosophers too, leaving behind a haze
    of portentous meaning,
like a classical name dropped in a student's sonnet.

But he was not a mere student, he was the Chief,
    the one who said,
quoting another classic after the first A-bomb sucked
    the desert up into a skyscraping mushroom:
"Now I am become Death, destroyer of worlds."
Was he warning us all including himself of the stakes
    of splitting atoms,

of presuming to command godlike forces that were
   ungodly real?
Down at ground zero, Oppie might have recalled
   Alfred Nobel's hope
that dynamite was so mighty it would end all war
   forever.

2.

We are Americans, casual, slangy, unhistorical,
so why not simply call it Doomsday, or if you want
the incense of sacred portents dub it Apocalypse, or
Armageddon. Or give it a name all its own,
MOAB, the Mother of all Bombs, a name
from the street, and a reference to biblical
Moab, son of Lot by his daughter, a child of sin.

Another commentator says maybe Oppie wanted
complementarity, as defined by Bohr, the dual
nature of energy/matter, both wave and particle,
particle and wave, yang and yin, west and east,
white and black, resurrection and death, evil
and good, all the inseparable Siamese twins.

Even with a poet's or physicist's license, naming
it Trinity doesn't anticipate the fate of two cities,
two pyres, two hundred thousand snuffed to
prepare the way for a brave new world by
obliterating the cringing old one. That can't
be what Oppenheimer so vaguely meant.

Batter my heart, etcetera, shifts from mind to
emotion, echoing Bunyan's Pilgrim's embrace of
his own damnation. *Enthrall and ravish me*,
Donne commands the Three Headed One,
and have I mentioned how un-American all this
is? We're the innocents abroad, folks on holiday,

kids at play, building a nice place to raise a family,
not some guilt-wracked, self-abusing misanthropic
scientist-saint quoting the Bhagavad Gita.

      3.
"There he was, you know, with his hat.
You've seen pictures of Robert's hat,"
Rabi described Oppenheimer after the test
at Trinity. "His walk was like High Noon,
this kind of strut. He'd done it."

Now I blessed the condition of the dog or toad,
said Bunyan's Pilgrim, *for I knew they had no soul
to perish under the everlasting weight--*

(All sing: "Here I come to save the day!
My name is Mighty Mouse; I'm on the way!")

*--and though I saw this, felt this, and was broken
to pieces with it, yet that which added to my sorrow was--*

(Chorus: "Here he comes to save the day!
His name is Mighty Mouse; he's on the way!")

*--that I could not find with all my soul that I did desire
deliverance.*

"We saw the whole sky flash with unbelievable brightness
in spite of the very dark glasses we wore."

"The thing that got me was not the flash but the blinding
heat of a bright day on your face in the cold desert morning."

"It blasted, it pounced, it bored its way right through you.
It was a vision which was seen with more than the eye.
It was seen to last forever."

"Partially eviscerated dead wild jack rabbits were found more than eight hundred yards from zero."

4.

They would have done it
so we have to do it, yes.
I would have done it,
worn the hat, strutted,
named it something, named
it something signifying
awe, hope, reverence,
fear, doubt, majesty,
power, power, power.

Yes, I would have done it, yes,
certain, all but certain I was
innocent, guilty of being
complementarily human,
mortal, envious of gods,
of power, apologizing to
the cow while carving
its steak, "How delicious!
I hope it doesn't hurt too much."

Vietnam Memorial

As I saw myself approaching in the
black granite mirror, I felt a definite
reverence rising in my gut but wasn't

prepared for so much emotion.
I stopped and hung back at a distance
feeling I hadn't the right like those

up close to get so close, as if this
distance between me and the black
slab was my opposition to the war

the names on it died in,
that to come here now to look,
to honor them, was a hypocrisy

or had something in it of the voyeur.
My opposition cost me nothing.
By chance, I hadn't been called.

There was no jail, no flight to Canada,
no lost time, no disruption of life.
Not like Steve who left part of himself

there or Bob's brother whose name is here
or Chris who had to have his conscience
examined by a board and received

his hometown's opprobrium for refusing
to fight (it's what I'd have done), and
I hadn't exactly confronted my luck before.

It seems to be written in the names
on the black slab; their enlistment
or conscription cost them all.

In exchange for the rest of their lives,
forfeited to stop dominoes from falling,
they got a name etched in black granite,

like the one pressed hard under the thumb
of the middle-aged man I'm staring at now.
I say middle-aged but he looks like a kid

made up to look old; gray ponytail with
bandana, jeans and boots, earring and
shades, a time traveler from the sixties,

back to greet a buddy, show him the lines
cut in his cheeks, in search of the lost time
together. Another name's female relation

stands in front of him, her head angled
in thought: Who was this kid for God's sake?
While the kid was in Nam, John Henry

and I sat in a darkened room in lower
Manhattan watching a film about a boy
who got napalmed. It took more than

a year for the burns to heal, another
to relearn how to walk. Just before
we went out blinking into the sunlight

the boy, now ten, got hit by another
American bomb and was melted again.
John Henry and I went to a bar and

drank a beer without conversation.
In the museum a ways up the Mall
are rows of busts, anonymous heads

sculpted by a German artist. They look
as if he put them in an oven to melt;
after the features ran together he took

them out and froze them. The lopsided
crania, mounted on the stump of their
necks, look down on us magisterially,

their melted mouths open to scream
or moan or cry out, to tell us what's
been done to them, what they've seen.

        2.
There's no grandeur here, just as critics
of Maya Lin's horizontal design said;
you don't snap to attention while

the Marine Hymn sings in your ears.
This is Taps. Instead of commanding
you to step back and look up, it pulls

you toward it, bowing your head to read
the names. The emotion I felt at first
sight surges up again when I'm finally

close enough so the names are legible,
and once I begin reading I feel compelled
to read another, another, another,

as if there is someone I'm looking for,
a name I'll recognize with a shock,

a forgotten classmate, a guy from

the neighborhood. Maybe I want to hear
the variety of origins, to savor the warm
melting pot of Hollywood war films.

Jack, whose family is Slovak, said after
visiting D.C., "You come away feeling
more patriotic. You really do, you know?

"All those monuments and memorials
make you feel something." We are
the ones who can feel something.

We are the unnamed, not yet set in stone,
free to live out our unfulfillable dreams,
free to oppose wars fought so dominoes

won't fall, free to come and stand in
front of heroes and grunts, the dutiful,
the unlucky who died for a mistake,

their monument tucked into a berm,
a bunker, a grave. We're free to leave too,
the names dissolving into the stream of

consciousness I wade away in, blinking
in the sunlight as my eyes turn from
the black granite wall to the bright

white distant obelisk climbing the sky
with such sheerness, as if it would
deny gravity, deny everything.

lower case man

he is the lower case man, he is dressed
in a new borrowed uniform, a neat fitting
leather flight jacket. he is the mannequin
of male fantasy, the one who wishes

to be adored as larger than ordinary life,
to be bronzed as a Hero. he is the one
whose headpiece is filled with tales
starring upper case virtues: Courage

and Valor and Honor. he is the one who
dreams a finger of God has singled him
out, anointing him as the one whose gift
is so great it can be parceled out among

thousands of proxies who fly off to
do what he would do too if he were
not fated to be the lower case man.
he is the one who stands proud and

tall at the dedication of new buildings,
before the kickoff at football games,
on the holidays to honor dead veterans
when the national anthem is played.

he is not like the upper case men,
the ones who volunteered, the ones
who did not have other priorities; nor
is he like the ones who could not avoid

going, who were not so precious to
the nation that their bodies must be

kept from harm, so he might perform
a higher calling than being shot at

or blown up, and mimic the image of
upper case virtue on those occasions
when the Star Spangled Banner must be
played and spine-tingled civilians salute.

Already Dead

Duch, pronounced doik in Khmer,
in the dock for killing fourteen thousand
in the prison he ran during the reign
of the Rouge, claims he was guilty,
    but not culpable:
"If I disobeyed orders, they
    would have killed me," he says.

Dry-eyed in court, he wept in the video
of his confession, interrupting his account
"with a bark like a seal," said the reporter.
What had the seal done?

"I killed you already," says Duch in the dock
to a man who accuses him. "You cannot testify,
you cannot say what was done because you
    are already dead," Duch repeats.
"How can you not understand? You cannot speak,
    you are already dead."

A woman testifies that when she was a girl
Duch beat her two uncles with a steel rod,
under a tree, until they were dead.

She too cannot be here because, "All children
who came in with their families were killed,"
    says Duch in the dock.
"The dead cannot speak because they are
    already dead."

Duch is to blame for obeying, he weeps, or else
he too would be already dead like the ones who

can't testify because if they say they were in
Duch's prison they are already dead.
How can anyone not understand?

One Three Hundred-Millionth

As an American, I must be at least one
three hundred-millionth responsible for
the murders of the sleeping Afghans
by the deranged G.I. He's the decorated
soldier we read about, husband, father,
on his fifth tour, passed over for first
sergeant but not a problem guy, the story
assures us. One night he goes psycho from
the stress of war and starts shooting civilians.

Just what is a crime in a war zone? For
that matter what defines a war zone?
If we invade your country it becomes
a zone of war and your laws don't apply.
Our military brings its law along with
guns. Right and wrong get twisted in
a war zone. We all know that, we're
grown-ups here. Let's not wet our pants
over what is, no matter how regrettable,
inevitable in a zone of war.

All this will look different in five, ten years
(except to a few surviving orphaned Afghans).
Sergeant Bales will be in jail, or out, no longer
nuts. Or nuts forever. There won't be any
PR problem, and my responsibility will
have dwindled down to even less than one
part in three hundred-million, very little
guilt even for fifteen murders. Still,
fifteen's a lot. I wonder what it's like.
POP.
POP.

POP.
Just like that, one after another.
POP.
POP.
Does it get boring, repetitive, just something
to get done?
POP.
POP.
POP.
POP.
Are they all the same? Afterwards they are. Warm
bodies turning cold.
POP.
POP.
Are you keeping track? How many left to go?
POP.
POP.
Once you've begun, how do you decide enough's
enough?
POP.
Just one more for luck. You there--
POP.
It's easy to be clever about homicide.
What if they were kisses?
KISS.
KISS.
KISS.
You get the idea. If you did something like this
in a war zone they'd think you'd gone psycho.
KISS.
KISS.
KISS.
KISS.
Would I get one three hundred-millionth of the credit
for kissing fifteen Afghans?

KISS.
KISS.
Afterwards they're a little confused. Kissed by a guy with a gun. Weird.
KISS.
Just one more.
POP.
No, no--
KISS.

Super Bowl XLV

All our histories have converged at this point,
the ninety-two players, the coaches, officials,
the owners, the television crews and the fans
packed into Jerry Jones' Ego Dome--even his

self-regard is honed down to this moment--
and the viewers at home, at parties and bars
around the world, and the soldiers in Afghanistan
taking a break from being shot or blown up by

the Taliban, the devout foe of the Super Bowl,
willing to die to defeat both teams and their
billion spectators in the annual rite celebrating
the market economy, the American-bred global

materialism Allah will soon destroy because
it is godless, blasphemous, and heretical,
a mortal insult to the true believer, even if Ben
Roethlisberger points his soiled index finger

toward the sky when he scores a touchdown
to honor his god and ask forgiveness for what
he did to a woman in the ladies room under
the influence of alcohol (from Arabic, al-kohl);

and even she, an unrequited victim of football,
will be unable not to have some resented part
of her awareness focused on the moment when
the camera's eye unites our histories at kickoff.

Could a single blow be more momentous?
Down in the Dome the panoply designated by

Roman numerals conjures up Hollywood images
of the Colosseum, of thundering chariots and

the sweaty, clenched jaw of Charlton Heston, of
an Empire spread from Gaul to the Euphrates,
pre-figuring another from Montezuma to Tripoli.
TV is our host: after recaps of the previous season,

bios of players, predictions of experts, recitation
of the Declaration of Independence by choirs of
real folk, the national anthem sung by a pop star--
after hours of desultory foreplay, as if we trembled

to approach the immensity of the unleashed event--
it actually begins. The cleated, leather-clad foot
smacks the inflated bladder wrapped tight in the
skin of a pig, and Time restarts. My new heart valve

is made from a sacrificed pig too, and like billions
of others it surges with fresh blood as I watch
the arc of the ball flying end over end, dropping
down toward the helmeted, golden-panted player,

with Arabic numerals on his shirt so everyone
knows who he is. But we know who he is:
he is Will and Purpose and Sacrifice, he has trained
since childhood to receive this inflated object of our

world's attention in his muscled Superman's arms,
running up the field, dodging the maniacal, equally
muscled tacklers in their own golden pants. After
what feels like a whole year of waiting, the long

prologue is finally done, and with breaks for extra-
vagantly produced videos--the art form our

tribute pays to exalt the Gross National Product--
we are already leaving the new beginning behind.

In the conjunction between what just happened and
what we anticipate--the seamless cleavage where
time is restarted again and again--the intricately
diagrammed executions of force and gracefulness

explode. Although each is replayed instantly in
teasing previews of immortality, few will be able
to recall them a year from now, or even tomorrow.
The Super Bowl is not to be remembered but re-

enacted. Does one recall the taste of the wafer,
the wine, the prayer of blessing, the pastor's face?
Next year we'll kick off the forty-sixth Armageddon,
our new bets teed up with the ball, each one different

from this year's, yet as identical as a clone. When
the foot smacks the patiently waiting ball, it will be
just like this, the throbbing we're feeling right now,
the world rapt to see which colored jersey will win.

ately understood by the person who, by the way, need not agree with him in what he says, or believes he says, or wishes to say. The exteriority of language would be obvious since, in the very moment that I say what is *given* to be said, I could, at the same time, say other things ; and even if I express myself as *sincerely* as possible, sincerity itself is only a quality in my use of language, not the interior of the feeling, which remains evasive, or maybe even inexpressible. I say *I love you.* It’s everybody’s word ; and this word, because of its specific generality, can bear the nuances of my feeling toward someone. But this word does not necessarily state my feeling : it conveys it imperfectly ; it conveys, perhaps despite me, what I would not say, or conveys what I can be lying to myself about. There is a kind of pathos in language, which we can observe constantly : to speak is always to say more, to say less, or to say something different from what one would like, what one must say.

4. Friends, Others

115

The Unadvertised End

Things shrink
they flatten
they sink,
friends leave without saying goodbye.

I walk the dog
under the cloud of their laughing
confident faces,
a balloon hissing air.

Lily

On an August afternoon, a perfect Sunday
    summer afternoon,
all the insects with appetites for humans dozing
    or out of season,
long-legged, bandana'd Jeffrey strolls the aisles
    of our perennial garden,
graceful as a mantis, a dancer, a natural
    gentleman,
carrying his illness as lightly as a title, hardly
    there at all,
not today, not on this perfect Sunday summer
    afternoon.

Down past Hippo Rock around the apple tree
    he strolls, the cultivated growth
of blooming plants arranged to beguile the eyes
    the nose,
the tingling limbic system. A gifted audience,
    one with perfect pitch,
he stops mid-aisle before an Oriental lily, the sole
    surviving one.
Rapt, he studies it. Jeffrey knows his kin; the kind
    who hurl themselves
onstage and perform unblushingly for us to leave
    or take.

It's commitment is replete, yet also just--as right
    as justice,
I mean to say--bigger than his hand, pollen-yellow,
    edged in red,
attended by choruses of phlox, pink and white, and
    mascara'd black-eyed Susans,

the lily stands halfway up his chest, its blossom tilted
   toward his face.
Jeffrey gapes, pries his senses open wider and I hear
   him cry:
"Look at it! Look at it--it's incredible! It's absolutely
   incredible!"

I do look. I look at him. I look at the lily looking
   at him,
the two outrageous creations of nature in praise
   of each other.

Bullshit

"It's all bullshit," said Annabel,
    far from any kingdom, at sea.
Her husband's been sick,
    she's been through a lot.
"No, it's not," I said, defending reality politely,
    socially. "Not totally. It's not totally bullshit."
"Yes, bullshit," she insists, far at sea.

We get glimpses, echoes, in music, in math,
    in phrases like
In the beginning was the Word, whatever that
    means to an organism who can't read.
Like ravens we're too smart for our fate,
    too sentient for protoplasm,
too stupid to feel how our atoms are
    pixeled into the cosmos.
If the Golden Section had a place
    in our hearts,
if Fibonacci's Progression tingled up
    our spine,
if the faint radiation left over from the Big Bang
    (everything's afterbirth),
lit us up like *Missa Solemnis* or
    Climb Every Mountain,
if our brains were bigger, or smaller,
    or finer,
we could lie down and surrender to eternity
    with a smile.

Lie down?
Through that dozing eye we can see the step
    by step by step evolved reason why nature

  requires us to endure bullshit:
so we don't recline with a sigh and give up.
To be a fungus or a god is not too bad, it's here
  in between where it's nasty.
Priests call it a test of faith, singers exploit it for songs,
  but to be one lone body and soul
stuck in sickness is not poetic or holy.
  It's an obscenity, it's bullshit.

If we ever learn the trick of managing sentience
  so the body isn't tortured,
our descendants may look back and pity us,
  proud of the ones who suffered most,
the way we honor slaughtered warriors or
  crucified saints.
Tortured obscenely by man or disease, who wouldn't
  prefer to skip the whole trip,
the castaway lovers glug glug gluging at sea
  while the once-healthy,
the strong, smart, meltingly loved human being is
  turned into shit,
transformed into something like shit.

Happy Birthday, Josef

I don't really think about Joe's mortality,
what it means to be so chronically ill,
to have no end in sight but The End
(not that he ever looks; he's never had

the luxury). Even at my age you don't
think it will happen to you, an assumption
as natural as a turtle's shell, with amnesia
annulling the memory of pain. Joe himself

never thought anything could hurt him,
not after escaping home, his father's wrath,
violence, humiliation; even labor camp and
war and all the rest would not harm him.

Anyone who could survive his life had
slipped fate's grip and was, in some way
denying doubt, immortal. Only now, eighty-
four today, shelled and tender, with multiple

agonies breaching amnesia ("It can't go on like
this," Joe said, baffled) does the vital illusion
begin to loosen, and the solid fact of nullification
emerges as the future of you, absent, eternal.

Friends' Sweaters

I wore Jeffrey's black cashmere to
the Christmas party and Robert's
baggy wool blend the next day
against routine December cold.
Neither liked winter, I recalled,
joining, weaving together, if you
like, dead friends by their sweaters.

The gifts from their widows were too big.
Jeffrey was size XL, reduced closer to L
by the ravage of disease. Ironman Robert
was in godlike, nearly immortal shape, as
if to illustrate the koan: a perfect day to die.

When everyone was young and Fox and I
were sharing the shack on the bayou in
Sarasota, we shared each other's clothes too.
You'd grab a shirt, a pair of pants, and sometimes
hurry out with the wrong wallet and drivers
license, swapping identities too. We barely
kept track of money between us; didn't share
women or sex, never touched in fact, and once
he borrowed my ten year old fifty-three
Plymouth and blew it up. "How'd you do that?"
I asked. "Throttle stuck," Fox said. "No shit,"
I laughed, the code between us cool, very cool.

In Santa Barbara when I hadn't seen him for
a generation, he said to his wife as he opened
the door, "Jesus, he's bigger than I am!"
Christ, Fox, I nearly blurted back, what the hell
happened to you? His face was pitted, striated,

knife-slashed with nicotine, his body shriveled
on a diet of cigarettes and wine. "I quit, but
I still like the smell," he said thanking me for
the bottle of Cutty Sark. "Lost fifteen pounds
in two weeks," he described the Shick aversion
treatment. "Drink-puke, drink-puke, they made
me go through it again, said I wasn't taking
it seriously," he chuckled, sipping ginger ale.

What he had taken seriously was his four
year old son with a lung problem refusing
to see his father in the hospital because
his father couldn't help. "I was pretty much
out of control for a few weeks, living on wine,"
Fox described his binge. He was that kind of
stoic; you could only hurt him through someone
he loved. I sipped a beer, we ate pizza and
talked family stuff, avoiding art, politics,
the meaning of anything. When he got up
to go to bed, I thought, now I can talk to
Carrie, hear the whole story about when
their son got sick and Fox went over the edge.
Instead she said, "You're going to bed already?
Your friend's only here for one night!"

One night driving on Tamiami Trail,
Fox said something that surprised me,
flattered me too. Fox meant it but
what could I do when I had no art,
no means, nothing but an ignorant
juvenile urge, an idea, mostly wrong.
We were emblems of a kind to the other,
one rampant, one couchant.

For a whole generation, radio silence.

Then Carrie found me at the end of
a wire stretched all the way across country.
"Could you call on his birthday, it would
mean so much--he talks about you all
the time." She exaggerated, but now I had
to call so I didn't disappoint her image
of him. When I drove away in my rental car,
I looked back and there was Fox in the drive-
way; he'd turned back too, and gave a little
wave--the only time he'd ever looked back.

I don't have anything of his now, nothing,
not even the gray and green landscape in oil,
the one he did in half an hour, a cool, fluent
abstract expression. It appeared as if by itself
and fit me so well I told Fox to hold on to it
till I had some money. He sold it for beer.

All three friends had "the dogmatic assurance,
which all men dislike in each other, which
nevertheless no man who is earnest may lack,"
in the formulation of John Oliver Hobbes,
whose original name was Pearl Craigie.
These stubborn unposturing males were
protective not uxorious, had tight confidential
bonds with their women, in the same weight
class, opposite-gendered best friends.

Carrie called a second time, sobbing, to say
Fox's gaunt, crosshatched face had dropped,
dead, while he sat at the wheel waiting to
pull into traffic. "He liked a lot of people,"
she said, "but he loved you." For the first
time I thought of the men I had loved,
the ones who loved me, inside some bubble

of mutual dogmatic assurance. The men
were as few as the women. You can't love
many, there isn't time. Then there's no
time, there's a widow, a hand-me-down
sweater, a vanished abstract expression.

Permission
(for A. and J.)

Like the ancient, primitive rite of suttee
you want to fall into the grave after him
to consummate the totality of your love.
This is your heroic instinct.
Once you gave your all for your art,
now it's for him, for the memory of him.
To continue to live now means there is
some of yourself you withheld from him,
kept back, apart, when he was here
among us, which you did not do.
As in Donne's *Ecstasy*, two became one
and like Donald Hall losing his perfect mate
the same way as you, nearly the same way,
nursing him was your greatest joy,
binding you tight in a trinity with a deadly disease.
The days when you fled to get away from the illness,
the imprisonment, the cough cough cough
driving him crazy too--those days,
to have one of them back, one of them,
even if you spent the day crying--
"It's harder for the caregiver," he told me,
failing himself because he couldn't
help you help him enough.
Any pleasure now, any relief is a lie,
a betrayal, it's simply wrong that
he should be gone and you here when
there is no way to live with him gone.

I know the temptation of this extreme emotion,
its logic, its necessity: you were a dancer,
classically trained, the Royal Ballet,

as severe as the Russians, dancing till
your toes bled, muscles on fire,
airborne with pain in homage to art.
If you are true, it demands this of you,
all you are, who you are, everything.
This is the meaning, the ordered meaning of art;
what you felt for him couldn't be anything less.
Because he would not pity himself
you feel it all now, all he denied,
the awfulness of it,
that something so vile,
the lowest form of existence,
could annihilate its very opposite.
For six years he suffered; it burnished
his character so it shone in his ruined body.
Diminished, he became spectral and radiant
like one of those figures from antiquity,
one of those classical figures
who is no longer real to us with our
cell phones, our flat screen TVs,
our medical science, our irony.
Even so, dying, no one could be
so ironic as him, so naturally
dignified, and so funny.
Physical, sociable, principled, driven,
a dreamer, he was a force sustaining you,
taking you upwards. We no longer believe
in an ordered meaning for things
but in its dispersion, perversion;
yet order and meaning coalesced
around him, his embodied significance.

When two are made one
if divided again
the one that is left is nil,

the remainder is totally nil.

2.

The last time I saw him we talked
of mortality. Not in plain words,
not with candor, but in WASPy code,
our kind of haiku where a word--
even an unspoken one--or a pause,
a glance, a chuckle, a reference
to something absurd, silly, or grave
could trigger a cascade of mutual thoughts.
It surprised me to be talking of death,
not because he denied its possibility
--not like Susan Sontag who forced such
a fiction on her intimates to the last breath--
but because it was Tolstoy's white bear
in the room with him always,
the enemy he would fight and fight
to the end but not dignify with a name.
It had hugged him hard a few months
before but he escaped, a miracle,
self-wrought, like one of Houdini's,
yet the bear--its agent I should say,
the corrupter of cells--could turn a body
against itself, against its own ruling intelligence,
causing a kind of pain a person who hasn't felt
hypertrophic pulmonary osteoarthropathy
cannot imagine exists. There are new ways
of saving lives, extending them, extruding them;
to get up from bed in the morning
he had to climb on the rack--
he could have lain there,
accepting its strength--
but did it by choice,
turning the wheel

with his own hand,
willing it to move.

On this particular day, the last
I saw him alive, his day had begun
with a turn on the rack
before the Oxycontin took hold,
and he greeted me without his usual
bone-crunching philanthropic grip,
shuffled swollen-legged across the kitchen
to brew coffee and said he'd been reading
his favorite, Dylan Thomas. Do not go gentle,
the lyrical green and gold secular hymn,
was there on the table, on his laptop between us,
and responding to the subtle,
the transcendently subtle, beseeching
look in his eye with its faintly amused
veil of puzzlement querying voicelessly,
I suggested that as much as I also
admired the brave valedictory song
there were other ways besides rage
to go into that goodnight.
What I was trying to say without saying it
was that even though we were teammates
he didn't have to be brave for me
or for an ideal,
one that at that moment did not signify.
His audience had been awed and sated
by his performance, and although it seemed
impossible for someone as vivid as him
to vanish from this raucous circus
into the silent drone of eternity,
it could happen. All things,
almost all things, can happen,
and what I was trying to do, so ineptly,

was give him permission, permission to exit,
sooner or later, from the excruciated,
colonized body hosting his enemy.
As I spoke, I heard the word acceptance
hovering over the laptop; I saw him nod,
acknowledging the wisdom of several
thousand years of Asian philosophy.
He was being polite.
It was not mine but his own
permission he needed to go
into that goodnight.

We had talked enough eschatology.
Now we talked books, sports, politics,
what his daughters were doing,
the antics of dogs, the prosy
sawdust of lumbering days. By now
he was vaguely dopey with drugs--
perhaps they had let him talk briefly
of mortality while easing its pain.
The drugs and disease had his voice too,
the deep Russian bass now a half-lisp,
but he owned, he wholly owned the Buddha
smile lingering on his colorless face
while we drank the coffee he so
graciously made and set down
in front of me at the kitchen table.

     3.
"Come quickly, he's dying!"
said your voice on the phone.
That was more than six months ago,
your half year of suttee, of days,
nights in flames, searing identical hours
and infinite minutes on the pyre.
In time the neurologists will detail

the way cells regenerate after the insult
caused by what laymen call grief,
how it alters their chemistry, making
their host rage that this cannot be;
yet it is, it is.
These chemical messengers are from
the same pharmacy that makes us love
so madly, that use us so carelessly for
their own purpose, leaving us to make
up the reasons why in the flames.

He showed death contempt
and earned permission to die;
cindered by loss past compensation,
you need permission to live.

Ex
(with apologies to K.C.)

She's a dangerous woman.
She spreads a kind of disorder
wherever she goes, sprinkling it
like a perfume over everything
with her wand, her fluttering fingers,
Keane-wide eyes so concerned, performing.
She loses things she borrows,
she loses her own things too.
She leaves the room and something
falls on the floor, a dish, a remark,
her laugh is breaking glass.
She killed her ex-husband
by passing through town thirty years later,
calling to say would you like to have
dinner with me and my husband?
A day of expectant fibrillation
created a clot which broke loose and
blocked his brain, knocking him dead.

I used to think it was sex because
she was sexy and knew how to use it
but now I think it's something almost
more potent, something--even she
doesn't know what it is. It isn't
voluntary, it's like the reverse
of wishing to help, a kind of
competitiveness to lay waste but
selectively (the rest is carelessness),
to topple the male, the rule of the phallus,
a desire to inveigle or beguile herself
into your sympathy, into your heart,

your liver, and eat it, eat it all, saying
no thank you, I'm not really hungry.
But only if you were a man, the kind
of man already eating his own liver,
eating it himself, all of it. Only then.

Hamish hadn't quit drinking so much
as he'd stopped temporarily
lost the taste for it
lost it to fear
afraid to think what was wrong
since he knew what it was
more or less
he knew exactly
a cardiac funk
fibers not twitching in sync
not pumping right
it could quiver a long time like this
it could form a clot
it could find its rhythm again too
healing itself except that
he wanted to see his Ex again
for complex psychological motives
as simple as loving her once so romantically
and liking her too and her saucy American wit
for his own part he knew he was charming
impossible needing somehow och we all know
the wayward ways of the heart
the hert
to revive some part of himself
left behind in her
still with her
still hers
it was all so wrought up
so Shakespearean she used to say

the size of his gloom his need
his used-to-be-called soul
and don't think I didn't know it too
Sunshine he liked to say cunningly
fount of homilies
life's expert on life
thrawn oracular soul
why do you think I sat that long morning
waiting not writing pen in hand sitting
aware of a particular cardiovascular trauma
I didn't need a professional diagnosis
for fuck's sake I'm a doctor mysel'
not enough oxygen in the blood
not enough blood in the ventricle
seventy years old for Jesus' sake
I still haven't grown up
another thing she knows about me
it won't come up over dinner
the four of us husbanding and wifing so affably
after the diffusing years
sitting in my little hut
my retreat
listening to my heart flutter
the wee bird trapped in my chest
I imagined the trip to the emergency room
on a Sunday
the practical fear in Molly-Wolly's face
the interview with the resident on duty
you can forget that dinner with your Ex
Sunshine we're going to admit you with
a potentially fatal cardiac condition
evaporating the chance for
a double date thirty years later
both of us immeasurably happier with
my drastically reduced romantic possessive

destructive hert-fucking thumb-sucking
pump trying to beat
in my chest
in my hut
in my home
in the glen
in Scotia-stan
so far from Ameri-stan

Missed the date with Ex anyway
reaching for a slice of toast
the glorious morning
the clot broke loose
I was deid before I hit the floor
not even time to think Shite!
she killed me

The Graph of Love

It was the prostate cancer dinner,
only victims and mates invited.
A lot of laughter, some bad jokes,
and the ghostly appearance of Sal's
indefatigable dad who had to have
sex every night no matter what
the docs did to his prostate--if we
needed a hero the old guy was the one.

After the food and wine things got serious.
Candace brought out the folded sheets of graph
paper tracking Tom's PSA over the years
and opened them up on the cleared table.
The line connecting the inked numbers started
neatly, on one trembling hopeful page, then
she had had to add, taped on horizontally,
another, another, another till the line
stretched across the width of the table,
zigzagging up and down but mostly up
with each event--diagnosis, treatment,
recovery, recurrence recurrence recurrence.
Tom was curious too; he hadn't really
looked at it before, the record Candace
kept tracking their enemy over the years.
When he leaned over to look the taped
paper crackled and rustled. We fell silent.
We were looking at the path her heart took
on its twenty-year journey across the dining
room table, and the last taped-on page
drooped over the edge toward the floor.

In ancient days, someone might have said

the gods saw how happy Candace and Tom
were and that's what started the trouble.
One of those envious female beauties, already
angry because her perfect marble nose had been
knocked off or she couldn't find her arms, saw
that Candace' happiness was much more
complete than any love she'd ever known
so she made the cells in one of Tom's crucial
male organs begin breeding wildly.
That tale makes a kind of classical sense,
but Tom has a more modern explanation:
Not wanting to lose his means of fulfilling
his love, he had begged the surgeon to cut
carefully, to spare the nerves sending
the message of love to his organ of expression.
Respecting Tom's desire too much, the surgeon's
caution may have exceeded his judgment and
a remnant of selfish tissue was left to spread.

Candace and Tom had a storybook love;
a life not charmed but blessed. When the line
stopped, Tom didn't curse any gods, blame
the doctor or even desire--he'd do it again
for love--but murmured, "Thank you,"
to his family leaning in close to hear.

Yet Again

Yet again the unbelievable actually happens:
stretching plausibility, the melodramatic author
    gives Werner a swoon
and shoves him off the roof to land head first
    on the conveniently placed slate slab below.
No, you say, it can't be!
Ahead I see the familiar shapes of what also
    will happen again.

When someone essential is snatched away
there are only a few ways you can respond.
No, there's only one way, one route,
a single series or suite to use the word
the scientists are so fond of these days,
one I've learned to loathe for its clubby
smugness and faux originality, the way
I loathe the bogus uniqueness of death.

We're all the same and there's no other
    way to feel about loss.
That cut-out in the landscape of life
shaped like so-and-so through which
one can see the absolute, the mere
    nothing of nothing
sucking out so-and-so with a whooosh--
along with a slice of your own self, soul,
whatever, as if it never existed--
and the anger (how could this be),
the stupefaction, the dumb grip
that squeezes you to a dry hanky....

Through it all winds this snake of incredulity:

it can't be/it is,
it can't be/yes it is,
it can't be/it will be just like this
and incredibly
you can't/no one can
you can't/no one can alter a thing.

As boggling as the incredible is,
some of the emotions seem to hover
   overhead,
lifted by laughter perhaps
because my whimsical pal
saw the world, so much of it,
   as a cartoon.
We're all funny characters striding
around in the wrong trousers,
all puffed up with ourselves--
a neat physical trick almost any human
   can do
(although men are so much better at it
   than women)
making us even funnier to look at
than if we remained normal size.
The other incredible thing about
   these inflated features
is that when it's someone else phiz
they're so amusing to look at but when
it's you--by that I mean me--
   it isn't funny at all.
Instead, it's the most serious thing
   in the world.
And since death is the other most serious
   thing in the world--

I lost track of what I was saying.

In this state of mind when the incredible
    happens
it happens I go blank frequently.
In this blank I go back to recall
    but it's not there;
instead the incredible is,
forcing the fact of itself on us
like a bored, bad-tempered host,
and now I remember again my pal's gift
for turning the seriously silly real world
    into a caricature,
for keeping our absurd puffed up lives
    within the twenty-four frames
per second we spend performing ourselves,
keeping each other amused, irreverently
    amused, till we're in tears.

Battle Fatigue

I'm trying to think of a new way to think
   about death,
to out-think its cliche.
I don't like the way its simple binariness
   controls my response.
Each loss is distinct,
each story ends differently yet the same,
leaving a different shaped hole,
each vanishing vacuums a resource
   from the same reservoir.

A psychologist studied how soldiers reacted
   when comrades died in their unit.
Besides the immediate sadness, depending on
how close a survivor felt to the deceased,
there was the drain on an individual's sense
   of mortality,
the assumption he would see home again, enjoy
   a life after war.
When a certain percentage of losses was reached--
   the number was about a third--
the sense in the squad or platoon switched from
   aye to nay:
I won't make it home, I'm a dead man.

I'm not saying that's what I feel; I'm saying
   that's what I feel.
I'm not saying peace is like war only slower, paler,
   less boring, less violent,
I'm saying because so many are gone from
   my unit
I no longer feel I'll see home again; if I do

   I won't know it's mine;
I'll sit on the porch, rocking and waiting,
   trying to think of
a new way to think about--

I can't think outside the dichotomy.
There is no outside, my mind can't go
   no place.
There's bustle and grief, a few laughs, and--

My mind can't go no place.

Unmoored

The scene is dawn, with fog. Sky
and water gray, a waistless panorama
from my vantage in a boat.
Or I am a boat, something small,
pram or dinghy, floating free.
It makes the merest motion on the water,
the lift and drop of tides
or just the action of my breathing.

I could also be a balloon puffed up with helium,
the string slipped from a child's hand and
vacuumed up up up by physics,
unobserved, a speck in space, lofting, weightless.

The sensation is not unpleasant,
so smooth in either medium,
although the rupture's huge--
No, not a rupture, nothing breaks;
a phase transition, sublimated state.

                    2.
Someone irreplaceable can die and
nothing happens, nothing changes,
as Waldo Emerson said when he lost his son:
I'm still here, the world's around, he's gone.
But Emerson is wrong to say the death
of someone loved made him stronger,
solider, more present--except the shock
(he liked to shock) is dead on right:
stoned, weightless, adrift in plasma
everything changes mass:
I'm too big, all else too small.
What's gone is some of the whatness,

the what's out there surround all tapered down.
One measures kids in pencil marks
as they grow up the wall;
the marks I see are moving down,
crayoned arcs around the globe,
the taste of sticky-sweet finger-sucking pity,
infantile self-love when whatever It was
It was boundless. I was going to fill it,
rising past all pencilled marks;
yet now the view is of an earth so small
and I am bigger way much bigger than I want to be.

I think this may be what Waldo meant.
I hope it doesn't mean if I live long enough
there will be only me, unmoored
by orders more in magnitude.

Therapy Dog

Would you like the volunteer to come in
and let her golden retriever greet you?
It always puts a smile on someone's face.

Funny how that works--the dog who licks
everyone licks your hand with its long
pink tireless tongue, and you smile.

You can't help it. Some get teary-eyed
and cry, "Look--he loves me!" Yes,
and No. God loves everyone.

Magic

I'm tingling, almost giddy with importance.
The rubber-gloved hands of the anesthetist
fly over me, tapping veins so fast I barely notice.
His name is Steve and this magician will be
    putting me to sleep.

My body's being traumatized to extend my life.
I'm immensely flattered by all this attention,
although I know they'd do the same for anyone
    with insurance.

"If I should die before I wake," the old prayer went.
I won't exactly be here for the big event: Insert
    a syncope, a pause, time-out.
The surgeon had a friendly cup of tea with Jane,
    then excused himself.
Now he's seen my heart, touched it, cut it, stitched it,
    made it stop, start up again.
Medtronic Inc. sacrificed a pig to make my brand
    new valve.
I come back from my artificial nap, giddy, thirsty,
    wounded.
The doc appears the next day, smiling, arms akimbo
    like John Wayne, boasting of his work:
"You're doing fantastic!"

They save your life routinely now;
Dad had his miracle, Mom's had two,
with Beth the magic failed. Playing mortal
games you can't win every time.
It's more like a second helping than a miracle.
No angels hover, no Mephistopheles appears

to make a deal. You just meet the wizard Steve
whose flying hands excuse you from the room;
you don't get to see the trick performed--
breastbone sawed in two, ribcage pried apart,
the secret pulsing heart exposed "to wind and
public gaze," in Dr. Gillies' playful phrase.
In fact your absence is essential;
if you should wake while you are
etherized upon a table and catch
the magician in the middle of
his act his magic disappears.

The little that we see can be enough.
The real trick is not to be disabled
by the sight. Pinker says our world
is statistically, historically, less violent
but you wouldn't think so watching
what a suicide bomb can do. We live
by impressions and illusions, not by
stats. Faulkner said you don't know
how much you can stand until you
have to stand too much. After magic
works a spell, then back to earth, awake.

Russian Poetry

I see a woman
dark haired husky voiced
her clenched fist wrapped
in the other hand pressed
against her breastbone
a grimace like orgasm
on her face.

She is so uncool.
Her whole fevered being cares.
Russia, her love, has done this to her,
done it for no reason, against reason,
the mother who squeezes her young
so hard they can't breathe,
drops them on the frozen ground cold
picks them up again clenched
to her breastbone weeping ice.

The woman, reciting her
aspirated zh's and krz's
is making a sound we can't make,
we giggling and snickering Americans.
Their alphabet, the unwritable Cyrillic
klutziforms, are hieroglyphs
representing this sound.

Someone said in yankee slang
those Ruskie punks will shoot you
just to see if their gun works.
The sound she is making is trying to fill up
the hole the Ruskie punk's bullet makes
when his gun works, the hole the fisherman

filled with vodka makes in the melting ice
when he disappears ass first in the cracking
spring thaw; her sound is Moscow, Leningrad,
Stalingrad squeezing the European invaders
so hard they couldn't breathe, dropping them
on the frozen ground cold beside the poet's
ancestors, beside her brother,
her husband, her father,
beside all the dead patriots and gulaged
enemies of the state weeping ice.

The country is so big
so cold, so fevered
so poshlosty and hamisch,
a mortal roulette played
to the sound of Rachmaninoff
and drunken vomiting laughter,
only her husky klutziform cries
can express it.

Compost Heap

The passion, my God, the passion!
Strange how embarrassing it is now.
Why should it be so? To be exposed for
having cared so much? That's a fault?

I looked like a fool, that's the fault.
To be so sucked in, to hurl myself so
heedlessly into the game. Some of
the famous quotations bubble up but

I'm ignoring them. I took my shot and
I'm not going to rewrite history just to
look dignified. I was anything but. I
was insane. It was the best I could do.

Given my talents and flaws, I was bound
to crash and burn. But by God I had my
foot to the floor! Succeed or die!
I did neither. But I tried. Now I go out

on a glorious October afternoon and
turn the compost heap. I could stop
and think about all I did wrong, all
the missed chances, the strange case

of mistaken identity I was performing.
All that seems tired, unwise. The green
passions are old, the sere reflections
are fresh. I no longer want to impale

myself on a project; I want to turn
the heap, get my sure work done. What

else could I want when I know there
won't be any reward, any sense of

completion lasting more than a day?
When I was a boy, before adolescence
and willful young manhood kidnapped
my green person, I enjoyed a wisdom of

self, an ambition to be whole, sufficient,
neither performing nor withdrawing. All
that got tossed overboard; I jettisoned a
few other things too, refusing (I imagined)

to play nature's pawn, arriving here just
the same. What gives pleasure now, before
I forget my own name, is what Whitman
called avowals, signs from those who

caught a spark or buzz from his lines
describing what it's like to be here,
alive, more than any one of us is, a leaf
of grass dropped on the compost heap.

Grunts, Clicks

Grunts, clicks, squeals, moans,
a few cuffs on the chops surely too--
all the first urgent ways of indicating
what you want or need, where to go,
what to do, look, come, don't do that.
It's pretty amazing to think such a crude
single-celled vocabulary evolved
into Latin, Swahili, Sanskrit and
Mandarin but you can do a lot
in two hundred thousand years.

The miracle of speech milled through
our daily voice undermines wonder.
Teevee, phone chat, rhetoric, official dicta,
instructional drone--all the handy noises
and a chorus of transcendently bored
Valley girl Whatevers betrays our own words.
In revenge they hide the truth,
become casuistical, misdirecting,
fusionless vectors disguising
heart speak and brain wave.

Bob, for one, is obsessed by
how glibly words lie
and likes to tell about when
he was young and didn't speak
for a year and a half.
He was at an age when
the casual travesties
adults live with by habit
choke a teenager's throat;
the visions of truth and

beauty he saw and heard
while under the influence
of recreational drugs
beggared speech too.

But we grow up.
We need words no matter
how we betray them,
no matter how they lie in our voice,
whisper their secrets below hearing.
We would pry them out of their shut jaws.
After all, the words were ours,
we made them up, didn't we?
Or is our abused precious language
the only one we could speak
with this brain, heart, larynx, tongue,
this home and history: dummies of
a mute master, a force, a notion,
a Whatever we can't describe, even name?

The In the beginning exhalation
jump-starting Time, mc squared,
these antics caught and released
in music or math--in music or math--
what am I saying? Who's writing
these swaggering lines? I should
cut and delete, inscribe only blanks.
Once I begin editing there's no end
but The End, the last word a rattle
or sigh, beyond speech, beyond
wonder, beyond our miraculous
twitter. And, really, who cares?
Angels would sing without words,
a melisma of tuning forks, any

gladness you like, the perfect
telepathies we must be missing.

Respect

It's hard to remember, sometimes,
that without The End we'd be
as indifferent as God paring
his fingernails unto eternity.
Love would be trivial too,
lasting for a forever so endless
all that swollen feeling would stretch out
to a flat line, and in a dozy wish
for something--anything--to interrupt,
we'd begin dreaming of the obverse
of our engraved steady state,
wishing to be stepped on
like an insect, just to see what
it was really like to be nothing, right now.

They aren't opposites, these two,
an equal and opposite pair,
being alive or being dead (an odd
contradiction itself);
this isn't matter and anti-matter,
two states balancing, canceling,
complementing each other;
you can't flip life on its backside--
legs wiggling in air or lying limp--
the antipode isn't a ghost or
an album of memory,
you don't find nothing,
no verb can locate it.
One is and the other is not,
and no matter how much you try
to wrap your mind around it,
cessation is somewhere outside experience.

It is everywhere outside experience,
the unbounded surrounding
our rushed finitude.

So we have to give death some respect
as the swap we make for meaning,
the condition of tasting significance,
right there next to nothing.
It's a clever tease to one's organism
to incite emotions we would never discover
immortally--to make us ache and sing
and weep--you'd almost imagine
there must be some anthropomorphic
audience enjoying our bloody opera.

Sensing the ones I've lost,
their lingering smear of vitality,
I keep in mind the sardonic solace
that loss makes poignance possible,
the kind of blasphemy Beth would commit
more nicely than me, yet irritating some
with her too gracious view of a tea ceremony
finale: an aroma wafting away, a hand letting go,
a shout in the street like Joyce's Dopplering God,
the fleet whisk of goodbye to the party behind.

www.ingramcontent.com/pod-product-compliance
Lightning Source LLC
Chambersburg PA
CBHW070851050426

42453CB00012B/2133